D0242342

SAY IT IN
CZECH

by Milan Fryščák

Assistant Professor of Slavic Languages
New York University

Dover Publications, Inc.

New York

Published in Canada by General Publishing Company, Ltd., 30 Lesmill Road, Don Mills, Toronto, Ontario.
Published in the United Kingdom by Constable and Company, Ltd., 10 Orange Street, London WC 2.

Say It in Czech is a new work, first published by Dover Publications, Inc., in 1973.

International Standard Book Number: 0-486-21538-5
Library of Congress Catalog Card Number: 76-173447

Manufactured in the United States of America
Dover Publications, Inc.
180 Varick Street
New York, N.Y. 10014

CONTENTS

CONTENTS

INTRODUCTION

The Czech language is spoken by more than nine million people of the Czechoslovak Socialist Republic living in the western and the central parts of that country (Bohemia and Moravia, respectively) which, under the recently introduced federative system, constitute the Czech Socialist Republic. It is very closely related to Slovak, the national language of the eastern part of Czechoslovakia—the Slovak Socialist Republic—so that this phrase book may also substantially facilitate communication in that area, inhabited by over five million people.

In its spoken form Czech has several dialects. Among them the Central Bohemian dialect (with Prague as its center) plays a preeminent role: it forms the basis of both the Standard Literary Czech Language (*spisovná čeština*) and the widely used Czech Common Interdialect, or Language (*obecná čeština*). Although certain differences between Standard Literary Czech and some varieties of the spoken language are by no means insignificant, they do not impede communication, for practically all segments of the population are familiar with Standard Literary Czech as well: in its written form it is the medium of most literature, and spoken it is taught in schools and used in instruction on all educational levels, in public lectures and church sermons, in radio and television, in theaters and motion pictures, and in official proceedings.

The standard literary language thus represents a linguistic code which in its use is not limited to a particular territory or social group but serves as a communication medium for all the population of Bohemia and Moravia. For this reason it is consistently used throughout this book. Only exceptionally are parallel words from non-literary varieties of Czech also supplied—words that are known in all or almost all dialects, and that, thanks to their brevity, successfully compete with the literary language equivalents (e.g., Czech Common Interdialect *baterka*, "flashlight," in place of Standard Literary Czech *kapesní elektrická svítilna*).

NOTES ON THE USE OF THIS BOOK

The material in this book has been selected chiefly to teach you many essential phrases, sentences and questions for travel. It will serve as a direct and interesting introduction to the spoken language if you are beginning your study. The sentences will be useful to you whether or not you go on to further study. With the aid of a dictionary, many sentence patterns included here will answer innumerable needs, for example:

"I want to speak [to the manager]." The brackets indicate that substitutions can be made for these words with the use of a bilingual dictionary. In other sentences, for the words in square brackets you can substitute the words immediately following (in the same sentence or in the indented entries below it). For example, the entry

I am looking for [my boy friend] my girl friend

provides two sentences: "I am looking for my boy friend" and "I am looking for my girl friend." Three sentences are provided by the entry

> I want to send this [by surface mail].
> — by air mail.
> — special delivery.

As your Czech vocabulary grows, you will find that you can express an increasingly wide range of thoughts by the proper substitution of words in these model sentences.

Please note that whereas brackets always indicate the possibility of substitutions, parentheses have been used to give brief explanations or to indicate words that can readily be omitted. The abbreviation "(LIT.)" is used whenever a literal translation of a Czech phrase or sentence is supplied.

You will notice that the word "please" has been omitted from many of the sentences. This was done merely to make them shorter and clearer, and to avoid repetition. To be polite, however, you should add *prosím* whenever you would normally say "please" in English.

You will find the extensive index at the end of the book especially helpful. Capitalized items in the index refer to section headings and give the number of the page on which the section begins. All other numbers refer to *entry numbers*. All the entries in the book are numbered consecutively.

PRONUNCIATION

CONSONANTS

Czech Spelling	*Transcription*	*Remarks*
c	ts	Like the *ts* in "*ts*etse."
č	ch	Like the *ch* in "*ch*ase."
ch	kh	Like the *ch* in Scottish "lo*ch*" or in German "a*ch*."
d' (also d in the combinations dě, di, dí) [the form of the capital letter is Ď]	dʸ	A very soft (palatal) sound; it can be approximated by articulating *d* with the tip of the tongue against the hard palate.
f	f	Like the *f* in "*f*or" (never as in "o*f*").
g	g	Like the *g* in "*g*ame" (never as in "*g*iant").

h	h	At the beginning of a syllable, like the *h* in "*h*and."*
j	y	Like the *y* in "*y*es."
ň (also n in the combinations ně, ni, ní)	n^y	Like the *ny* in "ca*ny*on," but more nasal.
r	r	A trilled ("rolled") sound, produced with the tip of the tongue.
ř	rzh	A trilled ("rolled") sound; it can be approximated by pronouncing the Czech *r* and *ž* simultaneously.
s	s	Like the *s* in "*s*un" (not as in "ro*s*e").
š	sh	Like the *sh* in "*sh*ade."
t' (also t in the combinations tě, ti, tí) [the form of	t^y	A very soft (palatal) sound; it can be approximated by

* Sometimes pronounced *kh* after a consonant or at the end of a syllable. Do not confuse this plain letter *h* with the use of the letter in the transcription combinations *ch, zh, ah, aͪ,* and *eͪ*, where it forms part of an entire sound and is not pronounced independently.

the capital letter is Ť]		articulating *t* with the tip of the tongue against the hard palate.
ž	zh	Like the *s* in "measure."

All other Czech consonants may be pronounced more or less like their English counterparts. It should be noted, however, that in Czech, unlike English, *p*, *t* and *k* are not aspirated, i.e., not pronounced with a puff of breath after them.

The letters *q* and *w* are not normally used in Czech, and *x* is very rare. In Czech spelling, *y* is used only as a vowel.

Very often the pronunciation of a consonant is modified by the consonant next to it (or at the end of a syllable). This will always be indicated in the transcription. For instance, *odpoledne* is transcribed as *AWT-paw-lĕd-nĕ* (not *AWD-*).

VOWELS AND DIPHTHONGS

VOWELS

Czech Spelling	*Trans- cription*	*Remarks*
a	ah	Like the *a* in "tra-la-la."
á	a̅h	Like the preceding, but more protracted.

e OR ě*	ě	Like the *e* in "bet."
é	eh	Like the preceding, but more protracted.
i OR y	ĭ	Between the *i* in "sit" and the *ea* in "seat" (not protracted).
í OR ý	ee	Like the *ee* in "green" (protracted).
o	aw	Like the *aw* in "seesaw," but not protracted and with more lip rounding.
ó	aw	Like the preceding, but protracted.
u	oo	Between the *oo* in "look" and the *oo* in "loot" (not protracted).
ú OR ů	oo	Like the *oo* in "fool" (protracted).

NOTE: A macron (long mark) over vowels in the transcription system used in this book always

---

* After the letters *b, f, p* and *v*, the letter *ě* is pronounced *yě* (like the *ye* in "yes"). See the section on consonants for its effect on preceding *d, n* and *t*. The combination *mě* is pronounced *mnʸě*.

indicates that such vowels are to be pronounced in a more protracted fashion. For instance, in pronouncing the vowel indicated by "a̅h," you should roughly double the time it takes you to pronounce the vowel indicated by "ah." In other words, "long" vowels in Czech are not fundamentally different in sound quality from the "short" vowels (compare English!)—they take longer to say.

DIPHTHONGS

Czech Spelling	Transcription	Remarks
aj	ah‿y	Like the *i* in "*i*ce."
áj	a̅h‿y	Like *ie* in "l*ie*" (a more protracted pronunciation of the preceding sound).
au	ah‿oo	Like *ow* in "c*ow*." Occurs rarely.
ej OR ěj	ay	Like *ay* in "d*ay*."
eu	ě‿oo	A combination of the two vowel sounds. No English equivalent. Occurs rarely.
ij OR yj	ee‿y	Like the *ee* in "gr*ee*n."
íj OR ýj	e̅e‿y	Like the *ee* in "gr*ee*n," but even more protracted.

oj	oy	Like the *oy* in "b*o*y."
ou	oh‿oo	Like *ow* in "sl*ow*."
uj	oo‿y	Like the sound in "ph*oo*ey."
ůj	o͞o‿y	Like the sound in "ph*oo*ey," but more protracted.

NOTES: (1) In Czech, *l* and *r* can also function as vowels; that is, they can occur in syllables without any of the vowels or diphthongs shown above: namely, when *l* or *r* is (1) between two consonants or (2) at the end of a word in a position following a consonant. Examples: *vlk* (wolf), *prst* (finger), *vedl* (he led), *kapr* (carp). In such cases *l* and *r* are pronounced much like the final sounds in the English words "bott*le*" and "butt*er*," respectively (but the *l* is not "swallowed" and the *r* is trilled or flapped in Czech instead of being a rumble in the throat as in English). This "vocalic" *l* and this "vocalic" *r* will be represented in our transcription by "ŭl" and "ŭr," respectively.

(2) Vowels at the beginning of a word are preceded by a "glottal stop" (a gulp-like sound formed in the back of the throat; it is heard, for instance, in the Cockney pronunciation of "better"). The glottal stop is not indicated in our transcription.

STRESS

The first syllable usually bears the strongest stress in Czech words. Despite this prevailing regularity, the transcription in this book prints the stressed syllable of words with more than one syllable in capital letters (e.g., *DAWB-rēe*). One-syllable prepositions bear a strong stress and form a group with the next word, which loses its own main stress. This is indicated in the transcription; for instance, *na dovolené* is transcribed as *NAH-daw-vaw-lĕ-neh.**

---

* Prepositions consisting of a single consonant (*k, s, v*) are pronounced together with the following syllable. This is indicated in the transcription; for instance, *s radostí* is transcribed as *SRAH-daws-t^{y}ee*.

EVERYDAY PHRASES
KAŽDODENNÍ RČENÍ

1. **Hello.**
   Dobrý den!
   DAWB-rēe děn!

2. **Welcome!***
   Vítáme vás!
   VĒE-tah-mě vahs!

3. **Good day.**
   Dobrý den! (on meeting a person)
   DAWB-rēe děn!
   Sbohem! (on parting with a person)
   ZBAW-hěm!

4. **Good morning.**
   Dobré jitro!
   DAWB-rēh YĬT-raw!

5. **Good afternoon.**
   Dobré odpoledne!
   DAWB-rēh AWT-paw-lěd-ně!

---

* Literally, this is "We welcome you!" If one person is doing the welcoming, the phrase would be *Vítám vás.*

6. Good evening.
Dobrý večer!
DAWB-r̄ee VĚ-chěr!

7. Good night.
Dobrou noc!
DAWB-roh‿oo nawts!

8. Goodbye.
Sbohem!
ZBAW-hěm!

9. See you later.
Na shledanou!
NAH-skhlě-dah-noh‿oo!

10. Yes.
Ano.
AH-naw.

11. No.
Ne.
ně.

12. Perhaps.
Možná (OR: Snad).
MAWZH-n̄ah (OR: snaht).

13. Please.
Prosím.
PRAW-s̄eem.

14. Excuse me.
Promiňte!
PRAW-mĭnʸ-tě!

15. **Thanks (very much).**
    (Mockrát) děkuji.
    (*MAWTS-kraht*) *D^yĚ-koo-yĭ.*

16. **You are welcome** (OR: **Don't mention it**).
    Prosím (OR: Rádo se stalo).
    PRAW-seem (OR: *RAH-daw-sě STAH-law.*)

17. **All right** (OR: **Very good**).
    Dobrá (OR: Dobře).
    DAWB-rah (OR: *DAWB-rzhě*).

18. **It doesn't matter.**
    To nevadí.
    taw NĚ-vah-d^yee.

19. **Don't bother.**
    Netřeba.
    NĚ-trzhě-bah.

20. **You have been very kind.**
    Je to od vás velmi milé.
    yě taw AWD-vahs VĚL-mĭ MĬ-leh.

21. **You have been very helpful.**
    Prokázal jste mi velkou pomoc.
    PRAW-kah-zahl-stě mĭ VĚL-koh‿oo PAW-
    mawts.

22. **It's a pleasure.**
    S radostí.
    SRAH-daws-t^yee.

SOCIAL PHRASES
SPOLEČENSKÁ RČENÍ

23. May I introduce [Mrs. Kovář]?
Dovolte mi, abych vám představil [paní Kovářovou].
DAW-vawl-tě mǐ, AH-bǐkh vāhm PRZHĚT-stah-vǐl [PAH-n^{y}ee KAW-vah-rzhaw-voh͜oo].

24. — Miss Vašek. — slečnu Vaškovou.
— SLĚCH-noo VAHSH-kaw-voh͜oo.

25. — Mr. Chytil. — pana Chytila.
— PAH-nah KHĬ-t^{y}ǐ-lah.

26. I am glad to meet you.
Těší mne, že vás poznávám.
T^{y}Ě-shee mně, zhě vāhs PAW-znah-vahm.

27. How are you (OR: **How do you do**)?
Jak se máte?
YAHK-sě MĀH-tě?

28. Very well, thanks, and you?
Děkuji, velmi dobře, a vy?
D^{y}Ě-koo-yǐ, VĚL-mǐ DAWB-rzhě, ah vǐ?

29. How are things?
Jak se (vám) daří?
YAHK-sě (vāhm) DAH-rzhee?

30. **All right** (OR: **Fine**).
(Velmi) dobře.
(*VĚL-mĭ*) *DAWB-rzhě.*

31. **So, so.**
Není to zvláštní.
NĚ-nʸee taw ZVLAHSHT-nʸee.

32. **What's new?**
Co je nového?
tsaw yě NAW-veh-haw?

33. **Please have a seat.**
Sedněte si, prosím.
SĚD-nʸě-tě-sĭ, PRAW-seem.

34. **It's a pleasure to see you again.**
Velmi rád vás opět vidím.
VĚL-mĭ raht vahs AW-pyět VĬ-dʸeem.

35. **Congratulations.**
Blahopřeji!
BLAH-haw-przhě-yĭ!

36. **All the best.**
(Přeji vám) všechno nejlepší!
(*PRZHĚ-yĭ vahm*) *FSHĚKH-naw NAY-lěp-shee!*

37. **Happy birthday.**
Všechno nejlepší k vašim narozeninám!
FSHĚKH-naw NAY-lěp-shee KVAH-shĭm NAH-raw-zě-nʸĭ-nahm!

38. I like you very much.
Mám vás velmi rád.
mahm vahs VĚL-mĭ raht.

39. I love you.
Miluji vás.
MĬ-loo-yĭ vahs.

40. May I see you again?
Můžeme se opět vidět?
MOO-zhě-mě-sě AW-pyět VĬ-dʸět?

41. Let's make a date for next week.
Udělejme si schůzku příští týden.
OO-dʸě-lay-mě-sĭ SKHOOS-koo PRZHEESH-tʸee TEE-děn.

42. I have enjoyed myself very much.
Velmi se mi tu líbilo.
VĚL-mĭ-sě mĭ too LEE-bĭ-law.

43. Give my regards [to your boy friend].
Pozdravujte [vašeho přítele].
PAW-zdrah-voo_y-tě [VAH-shě-haw PRZHEE-tě-lě].

44. — your girl friend. — vaši přítelkyni.
— VAH-shĭ PRZHEE-těl-kĭ-nʸĭ.

See also "Family," p. 211.

BASIC QUESTIONS
BĚŽNÉ OTÁZKY

45. What?
Co?
tsaw?

46. What is that?
Co je to?
tsaw yě taw?

47. When?
Kdy?
gdǐ?

48. When does it [leave]?
Kdy to [odjíždí]?
gdǐ taw [AWD-y̅ee̅zh-d ʸe̅e̅]?

49. — arrive. — přijíždí. — *PRZHĬ-y̅ee̅zh-d ʸe̅e̅.*

50. — begin. — začíná. — *ZAH-chee-nah̅.*

51. — end. — končí. — *KAWN-chee̅.*

52. Where?
Kde?
gdě?

53. Where is it?
Kde je to?
gdě yě taw?

54. Why?
Proč?
prawch?

55. How?
Jak?
yahk?

56. How long?
Jak dlouho?
yahk DLOH‿OO-haw?

57. How far?
Jak daleko?
yahk DAH-lĕ-kaw?

58. How much (OR: **How many**)?
Kolik?
KAW-lĭk?

59. How do you do it?
Jak se to dělá?
YAHK-sĕ taw DᵘĔ-lāh?

60. Who?
Kdo?
gdaw?

61. Who are you?
Kdo jste?
gdaw ystĕ?

62. Who is [that boy]?
Kdo je [ten hoch]?
gdaw yĕ [tĕn hawkh]?

63. — **that girl.** — ta dívka. — *tah D*ᵞ$\overline{EEF}$*-kah.*

64. — **this man.** — tento muž.
— *TĚN-taw moosh.*

65. — **this woman.** — tato žena.
— *TAH-taw ZHĚ-nah.*

66. **What is the matter?**
Co je (OR: Co se děje)?
tsaw yĕ (OR: *TSAW-sĕ D*ᵞ*Ě-yĕ*)?

67. **What do you want?**
Co si přejete (OR: Co chcete)?
TSAW-sĭ PRZHĚ-yĕ-tĕ (OR: *tsaw KHTSĚ-tĕ*)?

68. **What is this thing?**
Co je toto?
tsaw yĕ TAW-taw?

69. **Am I [on time]?**
Přicházím [včas]?
PRZHĬ-kha̅h-ze̅em [*fchahs*]?

70. — **early.** — brzy. — *BŬR-zĭ.*

71. — **late.** — pozdě. — *PAWZ-d*ᵞ*ě.*

TALKING ABOUT YOURSELF
OSOBNÍ INFORMACE

72. **What is your name?**
Jak se jmenujete?
YAHK-sĕ YMĚ-noo-yĕ-tĕ?

73. **My name is [James Ferguson] Margaret Ferguson.**

Jmenuji se [James Ferguson] Margaret Fergusonová.

YMĚ-noo-yĭ-sě   [dzhaymz   FĚR-goo-sawn]
MAHR-gah-rĕt FĚR-goo-saw-naw-vah.

74. **I am [21] years old.**

Je mi [jedenadvacet] let.

yě mĭ [YĚ-děn-ah-dvah-tsět] lět.

75. **I am an American citizen.**

Jsem americký občan (FEMININE: americká občanka).

ysěm AH-mě-rĭts-keē AWP-chahn (AH-me-rits-kaē AWP-chahn-kah).

76. **My address is 23 Hillside Drive, Denver, Colorado.**

Moje adresa je dvacet tři Hillside Drive, Denver, Colorado.

MAW-yě AHD-rě-sah yě DVAH-tsět trzhĭ HĬL-sah‿yd drah‿yv, DĚN-věr, KAW-law-rah-daw.

77. **I am [a student].**

Jsem [student (FEMININE: studentka)].

ysěm [STOO-děnt (STOO-děnt-kah)].

78. **— a teacher.** — učitel (FEMININE: učitelka).

— OO-chĭ-těl (OO-chĭ-těl-kah).

79. **— a businessman.** — obchodník.

— AWP-khawd-nʸeek.

80. What is your job?
Jaké je vaše zaměstnání?
YAH-keh yĕ VAH-shĕ ZAH-mn^yĕst-nah-n^yee?

81. I am a friend of Mr. Černý.
Jsem přítel pana Černého.
ysĕm PRZHEE-tĕl PAH-nah CHĚR-neh-haw.

82. He works for Čedok.
Pracuje v Čedoku.
PRAH-tsoo-yĕ FCHĚ-daw-koo.

83. I am here [on vacation].
Jsem zde [na dovolené].
ysĕm zdĕ [NAH-daw-vaw-lĕ-neh].

84. — on vacation from school.
    — na prázdninách.
    — NAH-prāhzd-n^yĭ-nāhkh.

85. — on a business trip. — na obchodní cestě.
    — NAH-awp-khawd-n^yee TSĔS-t^yĕ.

86. I am traveling [to Brno; to Bratislava; to Ostrava] to Prague.
Jedu [do Brna; do Bratislavy; do Ostravy] do Prahy.
YĚ-doo [DAW-bŭr-nah; DAW-brah-t^yĭ-slah-vĭ; DAW-aw-strah-vĭ] DAW-prah-hĭ.

87. I am in a hurry.
Mám naspěch.
māhm NAH-spyĕkh.

88. I am cold.
Je mi zima.
yĕ mĭ ZĬ-mah.

89. I am warm.
Je mi teplo.
yĕ mĭ TĔP-law.

90. I am hungry.
Mám hlad.
mahm hlaht.

91. I am thirsty.
Mám žízeň.
mahm ZHEE-zĕnʸ.

92. I am busy.
Jsem zaměstnán (OR: Nemám čas).
ysĕm ZAH-mnʸĕst-nahn (OR: NĔ-mahm chahs).

93. I am tired.
Jsem unaven.
ysĕm OO-nah-vĕn.

94. I am glad.
Jsem rád (OR: Těší mne).
ysĕm raht (OR: Tʸ Ĕ-shee mnĕ).

95. I am sorry.
Je mi líto.
yĕ mĭ LEE-taw.

96. I am disappointed.
Jsem zklamán.
ysĕm SKLAH-mahn.

97. We are [happy].
Jsme [šťastni].
ysmě [SHT^{y}AHST-n^{y}ĭ].

98. — unhappy. — nešťastni.
— NĚ-sht^{y}ahst-n^{y}ĭ.

99. We are angry.
Zlobíme se.
ZLAW-bee-mě-sě.

REQUESTS AND NEEDS
PŘÁNÍ A PROSBY

100. I want [a receipt].
Chci [stvrzenku].
khtsĭ [STVŬR-zěn-koo].

101. I need [a towel].
Potřebuji [ručník].
PAW-trzhě-boo-yĭ [ROOCH-n^{y}eek].

102. Give me [a bill].
Dejte mi [účet].
DAY-tě mĭ [OO-chět].

103. Come in.
Dále!
DAH-lě!

104. **Come here.**
Pojd'te sem!
POYT^y-tě sěm!

105. **Come with me.**
Pojd'te se mnou!
POYT^y-tě SĚ-mnoh‿oo!

106. **Come back later.**
Vrat'te se později.
VRAHT^y-tě-sě PAWZ-d^yě-yǐ.

107. **Come early.**
Přijd'te brzy.
PRZHEE‿YT^y-tě BŬR-zǐ.

108. **Wait a minute.**
Počkejte chvíli.
PAWCH-kay-tě KHVĒĒ-lǐ.

109. **Wait for me.**
Počkejte na mne.
PAWCH-kay-tě NAH-mně.

110. **Not yet.**
Ještě ne.
YĚSH-t^yě ně.

111. **Not now.**
Ted' ne.
tět^y ně.

112. **Listen.**
Poslouchejte!
PAW-sloh‿oo-khay-tě!

113. **Look out!**
Pozor!
PAW-zawr!

114. **Be careful!**
Opatrně!
AW-pah-tŭr-nʸĕ!

MAKING YOURSELF UNDERSTOOD
DOROZUMÍVÁNÍ

115. **Do you speak [English]?**
Mluvíte [anglicky]?
MLOO-vee-tĕ [AHN-glĭts-kĭ]?

116. **Does anyone here speak [French]?**
Je tu někdo, kdo mluví [francouzsky]?
yĕ too NʸĚ-gdaw, gdaw MLOO-vee [FRAHN-tsoh‿oo-skĭ]?

117. **I read only [Italian].**
Čtu pouze [italsky].
chtoo POH‿OO-zĕ [Ĭ-tahl-skĭ].

118. **I speak a little [German].**
Mluvím trochu [německy].
MLOO-veem TRAW-khoo [NʸĚ-mĕts-kĭ].

119. **Speak more slowly.**
Mluvte pomaleji.
MLOOF-tĕ PAW-mah-lĕ-yĭ.

120. I understand.
Rozumím.
RAW-zoo-meem.

121. I do not understand.
Nerozumím.
NĚ-raw-zoo-meem.

122. Do you understand me?
Rozumíte mi?
RAW-zoo-mee-tě mǐ?

123. I know.
Vím.
veem.

124. I do not know.
Nevím.
NĚ-veem.

125. I think so.
Myslím, že ano.
MǏS-leem, zhě AH-naw.

126. Repeat it.
Opakujte to.
AW-pah-koo‿y-tě taw.

127. Write it down.
Napište (OR: Zapište si) to.
NAH-pǐsh-tě (OR: ZAH-pǐsh-tě-sǐ) taw.

128. Answer "yes" or "no."
Odpovězte „ano" nebo „ne"!
AWT-paw-vyěs-tě „AH-naw" NĚ-baw „ně"!

129. What does [this word] mean?
Co znamená [toto slovo]?
tsaw ZNAH-mě-nah̄ [TAW-taw SLAW-vaw]?

130. What is this?
Co je toto?
tsaw yě TAW-taw?

131. How do you say ["pencil"] in Czech?
Jak se řekne česky [„pencil"]?
YAHK-sě RZHĚK-ně CHĚS-kĭ [„PĚN-sŭl"]?

132. How do you spell ["Jiří"]?
Jak se píše [„Jiří"]?
YAHK-sě PEE-shě [„YĬ-rzhee̅"]?

DIFFICULTIES
TĚŽKOSTI

133. Where is [the American Embassy]?
Kde je [americké vyslanectví]?
gdě yě [AH-mě-rĭts-kēh̄ VĬ-slah-něts-tvee̅]?

134. — the police station.
— stanice Veřejné bezpečnosti.
— STAH-nᵞĭ-tsě VĚ-rzhay-nēh̄ BĚS-pěch-naws-tᵞĭ.

135. — the lost and found office.
— oddělení ztrát a nálezů.
— AWD-dᵛě-lě-nᵛee̅ strah̄t ah NAH-lě-zoo̅.

136. — **the manager.** — vedoucí.
     — *VĚ-doh‿oo-tsee.*

137. — **your superior.** — váš nadřízený.
     — *vahsh NAHD-rzhee-zě-nee.*

138. — **a repairman.** — opravář.
     — *AW-prah-vahrzh.*

139. **Can you help me?**
     Můžete mi pomoci?
     MOO-zhě-tě mǐ PAW-maw-tsǐ?

140. **Can you tell me [that]?**
     Můžete mi [to] říci?
     MOO-zhě-tě mǐ [taw] RZHEE-tsǐ?

141. **I am looking for [my boy friend] my
     girl friend.***
     Hledám [svého přítele] svou přítelkyni.
     *HLĚ-dahm   [SVEH-haw   PRZHEE-tě-lě]
     svoh‿oo PRZHEE-těl-kǐ-nʸǐ.*

142. **I am lost.**
     Zabloudil jsem.
     ZAH-bloh‿oo-dʸǐl-sěm.

143. **I cannot find [the address].**
     Nemohu najít [adresu].
     NĚ-maw-hoo NAH-yeet [AHD-rě-soo].

Přítel and přítelkyně merely mean male and female friend, respectively, without the connotation of tenderness that "boy friend" and "girl friend" can carry.

144. **She has lost [her handbag].**
Ztratila [svou kabelku].
STRAH-tʸĭ-lah [svoh‿oo KAH-bĕl-koo].

145. **He has lost [his visa].**
Ztratil [své vízum].
STRAH-tʸĭl [sveh VEE-zoom].

146. **— his passport.** — svůj pas. — *svoo‿y pahs.*

147. **We forgot [our keys].**
Zapomněli jsme [klíče].
ZAH-pawm-nʸĕ-lĭ-smĕ [KLEE-chĕ].

148. **They missed [the train].**
Ujel jim [vlak].
OO-yĕl yĭm [vlahk].

149. **It is not my fault.**
To není má vina.
taw NĔ-nʸee mah VĬ-nah.

150. **I do not remember [the name].**
Nepamatuji si [jméno].
NĔ-pah-mah-too-yĭ-sĭ [YMEH-naw].

151. **What am I to do [now]?**
Co mám [ted'] dělat?
tsaw mahm [tĕtʸ] DʸĔ-laht?

152. **Let me alone!**
Nechte mě na pokoji!
NĔKH-tĕ mnʸĕ NAH-paw-kaw-yĭ!

153. Help!
Pomoc!
PAW-mawts!

154. [Call the] police!
[Zavolejte] Bezpečnost!
[ZAH-vaw-lay-tĕ] BĔS-pĕch-nawst!

155. Thief!
Zloděj!
ZLAW-dᵘay!

156. Fire!
Hoří!
HAW-rzhēe!

157. A difficulty.
Těžkost (OR: Nesnáz).
TᵘĔSH-kawst (OR: NĔ-snāhs).

158. An emergency.
Naléhavý případ.
NAH-lēh-hah-vēe PRZHĒE-paht.

159. A misunderstanding.
Nedorozumění.
NĔ-daw-raw-zoo-mnᵘĕ-nᵘēe.

CUSTOMS
CELNÍ ÚŘAD

160. Where is [the customs office]?
Kde je [celní úřad]?
gdĕ yĕ [TSĔL-nᵘee ŌO-rzhaht]?

161. **Here is my baggage.**
Zde jsou moje zavazadla.
zdě ysoh‿oo MAW-yě ZAH-vah-zah-dlah.

162. **Here is [my passport].**
Zde je [můj pas].
zdě yě [moo‿y pahs].

163. **— my identification card.**
— moje legitimace.
— MAW-yě LĚ-gĭ-tĭ-mah-tsě.

164. **— my health certificate.**
— moje zdravotní vysvědčení.
— MAW-yě ZDRAH-vawt-nʸee VĬ-svyět-chě-nʸee.

165. **— my visitor's visa.**
— moje návštěvní vízum.
— MAW-yě NĀHF-shtʸěv-nʸee VEE-zoom.

166. **I am [only] in transit.**
[Pouze] projíždím.
[POH‿OO-zě] PRAW-yeezh-dʸeem.

167. **[The bags] over there are mine.**
Tamta [zavazadla] jsou moje.
TAHM-tah [ZAH-vah-zah-dlah] ysoh‿oo MAW-yě.

168. **Must I open everything?**
Mám otevřít všechno?
mahm AW-těv-rzheet FSHĚKH-naw?

169. I cannot open [the trunk].
Nemohu otevřít [velký kufr].
NĚ-maw-hoo AW-těv-rzheet [VĚL-kee KOO-fŭr].

170. There is nothing here [but clothing].
Zde není nic [než prádlo].
zdě NĚ-nʸee nʸĭts [něsh PRAH-dlaw].

171. I have nothing to declare.
Nemám nic k proclení.
NĚ-mahm nʸĭts KPRAW-tslě-nʸee.

172. All this is for my personal use.
Tohle všechno je pro mou vlastní potřebu.
TAW-hlě FSHĚKH-naw yě PRAW-moh‿oo VLAHST-nʸee PAW-trzhě-boo.

173. I bought [this necklace] in the United States.
[Tento náhrdelník] jsem koupil ve Spojených státech.
[TĚN-taw NAH-hŭr-děl-nʸeek]-sěm KOH‿OO-pĭl VĚ-spaw-yě-neekh STAH-těkh.

174. These are [gifts].
Toto jsou [dárky].
TAW-taw ysoh‿oo [DAHR-kĭ].

175. This is all I have.
Toto je všechno, co mám.
TAW-taw yě FSHĚKH-naw, tsaw mahm.

176. **Must duty be paid on [these things]?**
Musí se platit clo za [tyto věci]?
MOO-see-sĕ PLAH-tʸĭt tslaw ZA-[tĭ-taw VYĚ-tsĭ]?

177. **Have you finished?**
Už jste skončil?
OOSH-stĕ SKAWN-chĭl?

BAGGAGE
ZAVAZADLA

178. **Where can we check our baggage through [to Bratislava]?**
Odkud můžeme odeslat naše věci jako spoluzavazadla [do Bratislavy]?
AWT-koot MŌO-zhĕ-mĕ AW-dĕ-slaht NAH-shĕ VYĚ-tsĭ YAH-kaw SPAW-loo-zah-vah-zah-dlah [DAW-brah-tʸĭ-slah-vĭ]?

179. **These things [to the left] to the right belong to me.**
Tamty věci [nalevo] napravo patří mně.
TAHM-tĭ VYĚ-tsĭ [NAH-lĕ-vaw] NAH-prah-vaw PAH-trzhee mnʸĕ.

180. **I cannot find all my baggage.**
Nemohu najít všechna svá zavazadla.
NĚ-maw-hoo NAH-yeet FSHĚKH-nah svah ZAH-vah-zah-dlah.

181. **One [of my bags] is missing.**
  Schází mi jeden [z mých (cestovních) vaků].
  SKHAH-zee mĭ YĔ-děn [zmeekh (TSĔS-tawv-nʸeekh) VAH-koo].

182. **I want to leave these bags here [for a few days].**
  Chci zde nechat tyto (cestovní) vaky [několik dní].
  khtsĭ zdě NĔ-khat TĬ-taw (TSĔS-tawv-nʸee) VAH-kĭ [NʸĔ-kaw-lĭk dnʸee].

183. **I have [a black trunk].**
  Mám [velký černý kufr].
  mahm [VĔL-kee CHĔR-nee KOO-fŭr].

184. **— a suitcase. — kufr. —** *KOO-fŭr.*

185. **— a package. — balík. —** *BAH-leek.*

186. **— four pieces [of luggage] altogether.**
  — celkem čtyři kusy [zavazadel].
  — *TSĔL-kĕm CHTĬ-rzhĭ KOO-sĭ [ZAH-vah-zah-děl].*

187. **Carry these for me.**
  Odneste mi tohleto.
  AWD-něs-tě mĭ TAW-hlě-taw.

188. **Take me to a taxi.**
  Zaveďte mě k taxíkovi.
  ZAH-větʸ-tě mnʸě KTAH-ksee-kaw-vĭ.

189. Follow me.
Jděte za mnou.
YD^{y}Ě-tě ZAH-mnoh‿oo.

190. Handle this carefully.
Zacházejte s tím opatrně!
ZAH-khah-zay-tě st^{y}eem AW-pah-tŭr-n^{y}ě!

191. What is the customary tip?
Kolik se obyčejně dává spropitného?
KAW-lĭk-sě AW-bĭ-chay-n^{y}ě DĀH-vah
SPRAW-pĭt-neh-haw?

192. The baggage check.
Stvrzenka od zavazadel.
STVŬR-zěn-kah AWD-zah-vah-zah-děl.

193. The baggage room.
Podej a výdej spoluzavazadel.
*PAW-day ah VĒE-day SPAW-loo-zah-vah-zah-
děl.*

194. The baggage checkroom.
Úschovna zavazadel.
ŌOS-khawv-nah ZAH-vah-zah-děl.

195. Porter.
Nosič.
NAW-sĭch.

GENERAL TRAVEL DIRECTIONS

BĚŽNÉ CESTOVNÍ INFORMACE

196. I want to go [to the airline office].
Chci jít [do kanceláře letecké společnosti].
khtsĭ yeet [DAW-kahn-tsě-lah-rzhě LĚ-těts-keh SPAW-lěch-naws-t^yĭ].

197. — to the travel agent's office.
— do cestovní kanceláře.
— DAW-tsěs-tawv-n^yee KAHN-tsě-lah-rzhě.

198. — to the Czechoslovak government tourist office.
— do státní československé cestovní kanceláře.
— DAW-staht-n^yee CHĚS-kaw-slaw-věn-skeh TSĚS-tawv-n^yee KAHN-tsě-lah-rzhě.

199. How long does it take to go [to Carlsbad]?
Jak dlouho trvá cesta [do Karlových Var]?
yahk DLOH_OO-haw TŬR-vah TSĚS-tah [DAW-kahr-law-veekh vahr]?

200. When will we arrive [at Brno]?
Kdy přijedeme [do Brna]?
gdĭ PRZHĬ-yě-dě-mě [DAW-bŭr-nah]?

201. Is this the most direct way [to Žilina]?

Je to nejkratší cesta [do Žiliny]?

yě taw NAY-kraht-sheē TSĚS-tah [DAW-zhĭ-lĭ-nĭ]?

202. Please show me the way [to the center of town].

Ukažte mi, prosím, jak se dostanu [do středu města].

OO-kash-tě mĭ, PRAW-seēm, YAHK-sě DAW-stah-noo [DAW-strzhě-doo MNʸĚS-tah].

203. — to the residential section.

— do obytných čtvrtí.

— DAW-aw-bĭt-neēkh CHTVŮR-tʸee.

204. — to the shopping section.

— do obchodní čtvrti.

— DAW-awp-khawd-nʸeē CHTVŮR-tʸĭ.

205. — to the suburbs. — do předměstí.

— DAW-przhěd-mnʸěs-tʸee.

206. — to the city. — do města.

— DAW-mnʸěs-tah.

207. — to the village. — do vesnice.

— DAW-věs-nʸĭ-tsě.

208. — to the country.

— ven z města (OR: na venkov).

— VĚNZ-mnʸěs-tah (OR: NAH-věn-kawf).

209. Do I turn [to the north]?
Mám odbočit [na sever]?
ma͞hm AWD-baw-chĭt [NAH-sĕ-vĕr]?

210. — to the south. — na jih. — *NAH-yĭkh.*

211. — to the east. — na východ.
— *NAH-ve͞e-khawt.*

212. — to the west. — na západ.
— *NAH-za͞h-paht.*

213. — to the right. — napravo.
— *NAH-prah-vaw.*

214. — to the left. — nalevo. — *NAH-lĕ-vaw.*

215. What [street] is this?
Jak se jmenuje tato [ulice]?
YAHK-sĕ YMĚ-noo-yĕ TAH-taw [OO-lĭ-tsĕ]?

216. How far is it?
Jak je to daleko?
YAHK-yĕ taw DAH-lĕ-kaw?

217. Is it near or far?
Je to blízko nebo daleko?
yĕ taw BLE͞ES-kaw NĚ-baw DAH-lĕ-kaw?

218. Can I walk there?
Dostanu se tam pěšky?
DAW-stah-noo-sĕ tahm PYĚSH-kĭ?

219. Am I going in the right direction?
Jdu správným směrem?
ydoo SPRA͞HV-neem SMNʸĚ-rĕm?

220. Please point.
Prosím, ukažte mi rukou.
PRAW-seem, OO-kash-tĕ mĭ ROO-koh_oo.

221. Should I go [this way]?
Mám jít [tudy]?
mahm yeet [TOO-dĭ]?

222. — that way. — tamtudy. **—** *TAHM-too-dĭ.*

223. Two streets ahead and then turn left.
Dvě ulice rovně a pak odbočit doleva.
dvyĕ OO-lĭ-tsĕ RAWV-nʸĕ ah pahk AWD-baw-chĭt DAW-lĕ-vah.

224. Is it [on this side of the street]?
Je to [na této straně ulice]?
yĕ taw [NAH-teh-taw STRAH-nʸĕ OO-lĭ-tsĕ]?

225. — on the other side of the street.
— na protější straně ulice.
— *NAH-praw-tʸay-shee STRAH-nʸĕ OO-lĭ-tsĕ.*

226. — across the bridge.
— na druhé straně mostu.
— *NAH-droo-heh STRAH-nʸĕ MAWS-too.*

227. — along the boulevard.
— na hlavní třídě.
— *NAH-hlahv-nʸee TRZHEE-dʸĕ.*

228. — between these avenues.
— mezi těmito dvěma (širokými) ulicemi.
— *MĔ-zĭ TʸĔ-mĭ-taw DVYĔ-mah (SHĬ-raw-kee-mĭ) OO-lĭ-tsĕ-mĭ.*

229. — **beyond the traffic light.**
  — za (těmi) dopravními světly.
  — *ZAH-(t*^{y}*ĕ-mĭ) DAW-p̄rahv-n*^{y}*ee-mĭ*
  SVYĚT-lĭ.

230. — **next to the apartment house.**
  — vedle (toho) činžáku.
  — *VĚD-lĕ (TAW-haw) CHĬN-zhah-koo.*

231. — **at the corner.** — (tamhle) na rohu.
  — *(TAHM-hlĕ) NAH-raw-hoo.*

232. — **in the middle of the block.**
  — uprostřed domovního bloku.
  — *OO-praw-strzhĕt DAW-mawv-n*^{y}*ee-haw*
  BLAW-koo.

233. — **straight ahead.** — přímo před námi.
  — *PRZHĒE-maw PRZHĔD-nah-mĭ.*

234. — **back.** — vzadu za námi.
  — *VZAH-doo ZAH-nah-mĭ.*

235. — **inside the station.**
  — uvnitř stanice.
  — *OO-vnĭtrzh STAH-n*^{y}*ĭ-tsĕ.*

236. — **near the square.** — poblíž náměstí.
  — *PAW-blēesh NĀH-mn*^{y}*ĕs-t*^{y}*ee.*

237. — **outside the lobby.**
  — (venku) mimo vestibul.
  — *(VĚN-koo) MĬ-maw VĚS-tĭ-bool.*

238. — **at the entrance.** — u vchodu.
 — *OO-fkhaw-doo.*

239. — **opposite the park.** — naproti parku.
 — *NAH-praw-tʸĭ PAHR-koo.*

240. — **beside the school.** — vedle školy.
 — *VĚD-lě SHKAW-lĭ.*

241. — **in front of the monument.**
 — před pomníkem.
 — *PRZHĚT-pawn-nʸēe-kěm.*

242. — **in the rear of the store.**
 — v zadní části obchodu.
 — *VZAHD-nʸēe CHĀHS-tʸĭ AWP-khaw-doo.*

243. — **behind the building.**
 — (vzadu) za budovou.
 — *(VZAH-doo) ZAH-boo-daw-voh‿oo.*

244. — **up the hill.** — na kopci.
 — *NAH-kawp-tsĭ.*

245. — **down the stairs.** — po schodech dolů.
 — *PAW-skhaw-děkh DAW-lōo.*

246. — **at the top of the escalator.**
 — nahoře, po pohyblivých schodech.
 — *NAH-haw-rzhě, PAW-paw-hĭb-lĭ-veekh SKHAW-děkh.*

247. — **around the traffic circle.**
   — kolem kruhového objezdu.
   — *KAW-lěm KROO-haw-věh-haw AWB-yěz-doo.*

248. — **over the exit.** — nad východem.
   — *NAHD-vee-khaw-děm.*

249. **Apartment house.**
   Činžák.
   CHĬN-zhahk.

250. **Factory.**
   Továrna.
   TAW-vahr-nah.

251. **Office building.**
   Budova s kancelářskými místnostmi.
   BOO-daw-vah   SKAHN-tsě-lahrzh-skee-mǐ
   MĒEST-nawst-mǐ.

BOAT

LOĎ

252. **When must I go on board?**
   Kdy se musím nalodit?
   GDĬ-sě MOO-seem NAH-law-dʸǐt?

253. **Bon voyage!**
   Šťastnou cestu!
   SHTʸAHST-noh_oo TSĚS-too!

254. **I want to rent a deck chair.**
Chtěl bych si pronajmout lehátko.
KHT^yĚL-bikh-sĭ PRAW-nah‿y-moh‿oot LĚ-
haht-kaw.

255. **Can we go ashore [at Bratislava]?**
Můžeme vystoupit při zastávce [v Bratisla-
vě]?
MOO-zhě-mě VĬ-stoh‿oo-pĭt PRZHĬ-zah-stahf-
tsě [VBRAH-t^yĭ-slah-vyě]?

256. **I feel seasick.**
Mám mořskou nemoc.
mahm MAWRZH-skoh‿oo NĚ-mawts.

257. **Have you a remedy for seasickness?**
Máte prostředek proti mořské nemoci?
MAH-tě   PRAW-strzhě-děk   PRAW-t^yĭ
MAWRZH-skeh NĚ-maw-tsĭ?

258. **Lifeboat.**
Záchranný člun.
ZAH-khrahn-nee chloon.

259. **Life preserver.**
Záchranný pás.
ZAH-khrahn-nee pahs.

260. **The ferry.**
Převozný člun.
PRZHĚ-vawz-nee chloon.

261. The dock (OR: **pier**).
Přístaviště.
PRZHEE-stah-vĭsh-tʸě.

262. The cabin.
Kajuta.
KAH-yoo-tah.

263. The deck.
Paluba.
PAH-loo-bah.

264. The gymnasium.
Tělocvična.
TʸĚ-law-tsvĭch-nah.

265. The pool.
Bazén.
BAH-zehn.

266. The captain.
Kapitán.
KAH-pĭ-tahn.

267. The purser.
Lodní pokladník.
LAWD-nʸee PAW-klahd-nʸeek.

268. The cabin steward.
Lodní sluha.
LAWD-nʸee SLOO-hah.

269. The dining room steward.
Lodní číšník.
LAWD-nʸee CHEESH-nʸeek.

AIRPLANE
LETADLO

270. **I want to make a reservation.** (LIT.:
     order an airplane ticket).
     Chtěl bych si objednat letenku.
     KHT^y*ĚL-bǐkh-sǐ AWB-yĕd-naht LĚ-tĕn-koo.*

271. **When is the next flight [to Vienna]?**
     Kdy je další let [do Vídně]?
     gdǐ yĕ DAHL-shēe lĕt [DAW-veed-n^y*ĕ]?*

272. **When does the plane reach [Brno]?**
     Kdy přiletíme do [Brna]?
     gdǐ PRZHĬ-lĕ-t^y*ēe-mĕ DAW-[bǔr-nah]?*

273. **May I confirm the reservation by tele-
     phone?**
     Mohu potvrdit rezervaci telefonicky?
     MAW-hoo PAW-tvǔr-d^y*ǐt RĚ-zĕr-vah-tsǐ TĚ-
     lĕ-faw-nǐts-kǐ?*

274. **At what time should we check in [at the
     airport]?**
     Kdy máme být [na letišti]?
     gdǐ MĀH-mĕ bēet [NAH-lĕ-t^y*ǐsh-t*^y*ǐ]?*

275. **How long does it take to get to the air-
     port from my hotel?**
     Jak dlouho trvá cesta na letiště z hotelu, kde
     bydlím?
     *yahk DLOH‿OO-haw TŬR-vāh TSĚS-tah
     NAH-lĕ-t*^y*ǐsh-t*^y*ĕ SKHAW-tĕ-loo, gdĕ BĬD-
     lēem?*

276. Does the plane stop en route?
Zastavuje letadlo po cestě?
ZAH-stah-voo-yě LĚ-tah-dlaw PAW-tsěs-tᵛě?

277. May I stop over (LIT.: **interrupt the flight) [in Olomouc]?**
Mohu přerušit let [v Olomouci]?
MAW-hoo PRZHĚ-roo-shĭt lět [VAW-law-moh‿oo-tsĭ]?

278. We want to travel [first class].
Chceme letět [první třídou].
KHTSĚ-mě LĚ-tᵛět [PŬRV-nᵛee TRZHĒĒ-doh‿oo].

279. — economy class. — turistickou třídou.
— TOO-rĭs-tĭts-koh‿oo TRZHĒĒ-doh‿oo.

280. How much baggage am I allowed?
Kolik si smím vzít s sebou zavazadel?
KAW-lĭk-sĭ smēēm vzeet SSĚ-boh‿oo ZAH-vah-zah-děl?

281. How much per kilo for excess?
Kolik se platí za kilogram přes váhu?
KAW-lĭk-sě PLAH-tᵛee ZAH-kĭ-law-grahm PRZHĚS-vah-hoo?

282. May I carry this on board?
Mohu si tohle vzít s sebou do letadla?
MAW-hoo-sĭ TAW-hlě vzeet SSĚ-boh‿oo DAW-lě-tah-dlah?

283. **Give me a seat [on the aisle].**

Dejte mi místo [vedle uličky].

DAY-tĕ mĭ MĒES-taw [VĔD-lĕ OO-lĭch-kĭ].

284. **What kind of plane is used on that flight?**

Jakého letadla se používá na tom letu?

YAH-kēh-haw LĔ-tah-dlah-sĕ PAW-oo-zhēe-vah NAH-tawm LĔ-too?

285. **Will food be served?**

Bude se podávat jídlo?

BOO-dĕ-sĕ PAW-dāh-vaht YĒE-dlaw?

286. **Is there bus service between the airport and the city?**

Je autobusové spojení mezi letištěm a městem?

yĕ AH_OO-taw-boo-saw-vēh SPAW-yĕ-nᵞēe MĔ-zĭ LĔ-tᵞĭsh-tᵞĕm ah MNᵞĔS-tĕm?

287. **Is flight [22] on time?**

Letí let číslo [dvaadvacet] bez zpoždění?

LĔ-tᵞēe lĕt CHĒES-law [DVAH-ah-dvah-tsĕt] BĔS-spawzh-dᵞĕ-nᵞēe?

288. **May we board the plane now?**

Můžeme už nastoupit do letadla?

MŌO-zhĕ-mĕ oosh NAH-stoh_oo-pĭt DAW-lĕ-tah-dlah?

289. From which gate does my flight leave?
Z kterého nástupiště odletí moje letadlo?
SKTĚ-reh-haw NAH-stoo-pǐsh-t^{y}ě AWD-lě-t^{y}ee MAW-yě LĚ-tah-dlaw?

290. Please call the stewardess.
Zavolejte, prosím, letušku.
ZAH-vaw-lay-tě, PRAW-seem, LĚ-toosh-koo.

291. Fasten your seat belts.
Zapněte si upínací pásy.
ZAH-pn^{y}ě-tě-sǐ OO-pee-nah-tsee PAH-sǐ.

292. No smoking.
Kouření zakázáno.
KOH‿OO-rzhě-n^{y}ee ZAH-kah-zah-naw.

293. An announcement.
Oznámení.
AW-znah-mě-n^{y}ee.

294. The stewardess.
Letuška.
LĚ-toosh-kah.

295. A boarding pass.
Palubní vstupenka.
PAH-loob-n^{y}ee FSTOO-pěn-kah.

296. The limousine.
Limuzína.
LǏ-moo-zee-nah.

TRAIN
VLAK

297. **When does the next train [for Pilsen] leave?**
Kdy odjíždí příští vlak [do Plzně]?
gdĭ AWD-yeezh-dᵘee PRZHEESH-tᵘee vlahk [DAW-pŭlz-nᵘĕ]?

298. **Is there [an earlier train]?**
Jede tam nějaký [vlak dříve]?
YĔ-dĕ tahm NᵘĔ-yah-kee [vlahk DRZHEE-vĕ]?

299. **— a later train. —** vlak později.
— vlahk PAWZ-dᵘĕ-yĭ.

300. **Is there [an express train]?**
Jede tam [rychlík]?
YĔ-dĕ tahm [RĬKH-leek]?

301. **— a local train. —** osobní vlak.
— AW-sawb-nᵘee vlahk.

302. **From which track does the train leave?**
Z které koleje odjíždí ten vlak?
SKTĔ-reh KAW-lĕ-yĕ AWD-yeezh-dᵘee tĕn vlahk?

303. **Does this train stop [at Kolín]?**
Zastavuje tento vlak [v Kolíně]?
ZAH-stah-voo-yĕ TĔN-taw vlahk [FKAW-lee-nᵘĕ]?

304. Is this seat taken?
Je toto místo obsazeno?
yě TAW-taw MĒES-taw AWP-sah-zě-naw?

305. May I smoke here?
Smím zde kouřit?
smeem zdě KOH‿OO-rzhĭt?

306. Will smoking disturb you?
Bude vám vadit, když budu kouřit?
BOO-dě vahm VAH-dᵞĭt, gdĭsh BOO-doo
*   KOH‿OO-rzhĭt?*

307. Open the window.
Otevřete okno.
AW-tĕv-rzhĕ-tĕ AWK-naw.

308. Close the door.
Zavřete dveře.
ZAH-vᵣzhĕ-tĕ DVĚ-rzhĕ.

309. Where are we now?
Kde ted' jsme?
gdĕ tĕtᵞ ysmĕ?

310. The conductor.
Průvodčí.
PRŌO-vawt-chee.

311. The gate.
Vchod.
fkhawt.

312. **A one-way ticket.**
Jednoduchá jízdenka (OR: Jízdenka „tam").
*YĚD-naw-doo-kh*a͞h *YE͞EZ-děn-kah* (OR:
YE͞EZ-děn-kah „tahm").

313. **A round-trip ticket.**
Zpáteční jízdenka.
*SPA͞H-těch-n*y͞ee *YE͞EZ-děn-kah.*

314. **A platform ticket.**
Peronní lístek.
*PĚ-rawn-n*y͞ee *LE͞ES-těk.*

315. **The railroad station.**
Nádraží.
NA͞H-drah-zhe͞e.

316. **The sleeping car.**
Spací vůz.
SPAH-tse͞e vo͞os.

317. **The smoking car.**
Vůz pro kuřáky (OR: Kuřák).
*vo͞os PRAW-koo-rzh*a͞h*-k*ĭ (OR: *KOO-rzh*a͞h*k).*

318. **The ticket office.**
Pokladna.
PAW-klahd-nah.

BUS, TROLLEY BUS, STREETCAR

AUTOBUS, TROLEJBUS, TRAMVAJ

319. **Where does [the streetcar] stop?**
Kde zastavuje [tramvaj]?
gdě ZAH-stah-voo-yě [TRAHM-vah_y]?

320. **How often does [the bus] run?**
Jak často jezdí [autobus]?
yahk CHAHS-taw YĚZ-dʸēē [AH_OO-taw-boos]?

321. **What [bus] goes to Strašnice?**
Který [autobus] jezdí do Strašnic?
KTĚ-rēē [AH_OO-taw-boos] YĚZ-dʸēē DAW-strahsh-nʸĭts?

322. **How much is the fare?**
Kolik stojí jízdenka?
KAW-lĭk STAW-yee YĒEZ-děn-kah?

323. **Do you go near Jungmann Square?**
Jedete poblíž Jungmannova náměstí?
YĚ-dě-tě PAW-blēesh YOONG-mah-naw-vah NĀH-mnʸěs-tʸēē?

324. **Will I have to change?**
Musím přestupovat?
MOO-seem PRZHĚ-stoo-paw-vaht?

353. **Are gas and oil included?**
Je už v tom zahrnut benzín a olej?
yě oosh ftawm ZAH-hŭr-noot BĔN-zeen ah AW-lay?

354. **Does the insurance policy cover [personal liability]?**
Zahrnuje pojistka [osobní ručení]?
ZAH-hŭr-noo-yě PAW-yĭst-kah [AW-sawb-nʸee ROO-chě-nʸee]?

355. **— property damage.**
— ručení proti škodám na majetku.
— ROO-chě-nʸee PRAW-tʸĭ SHKAW-dahm NAH-mah-yět-koo.

356. **— collision.** — ručení proti srážce.
— ROO-chě-nʸee PRAW-tʸĭ SRAHSH-tsě.

357. **I am not familiar with this car.**
Nejsem obeznámen s tímto autem.
NAY-sěm AW-běz-nah-měn STʸEEM-taw AH‿OO-těm.

358. **Explain [this dial].**
Vysvětlete mi [tento ciferník].
VĬ-svyět-lě-tě mĭ [TĔN-taw TSĬ-fěr-nʸeek].

359. **— this mechanism.** — tento mechanismus.
— TĔN-taw MĔ-khah-nĭz-moos.

360. Show me how [the heater] operates.
Ukažte mi, jak pracuje [topení].
OO-kahsh-tě mǐ, yahk PRAH-tsoo-yě [TAW-pě-
n^yee].

361. Are the papers in order?
Jsou dokumenty v pořádku?
ysoh‿oo DAW-koo-měn-tǐ FPAW-rzhaht-koo?

362. Will you pick it up at the hotel?
Vyzvednete si to v hotelu?
VǏ-zvěd-ně-tě-sǐ taw VHAW-tě-loo?

363. Bicycle.
(Jízdní) kolo.
(YEEZD-n^yee) KAW-law.

364. Motorcycle.
Motocykl.
MAW-taw-tsǐ-kŭl.

365. Motor scooter.
Skútr.
SKOO-tŭr.

366. Horse and wagon.
Koňský povoz.
KAWN^y-skee PAW-vaws.

AUTO : DIRECTIONS
AUTO : CESTOVNÍ INFORMACE

367. **What is the name of [this city]?**
Jak se jmenuje [toto město]?
YAHK-sě YMĚ-noo-yě [TAW-taw MNᵘĚS-taw]?

368. **How far to the next [town]?**
Jak je daleko do nejbližšího [města]?
yahk yě DAH-lě-kaw DAW-nay-blĭsh-shee-haw [MNᵘĚS-tah]?

369. **Where does [this road] lead?**
Kam vede [tato cesta]?
kahm VĚ-dě [TAH-taw TSĚS-tah]?

370. **Are there road signs?**
Jsou silnice označkovány?
ysoh‿oo SĬL-nᵘĭ-tsě AW-znahch-kaw-vah̄-nĭ?

371. **Is the road [paved]?**
Je ta silnice [asfaltovaná (OR: dlážděná)]?
yě tah SĬL-nᵘĭ-tsě [AHS-fahl-taw-vah-nah̄ (OR: DLA̅HZH-dᵘě-nah̄)]?

372. **— rough.** — hrbolatá. — *HŬR-baw-lah-tah̄.*

373. **Show me the easiest way.**
Ukažte mi nejsnadnější cestu.
OO-kahsh-tě mĭ NAY-snahd-nᵘay-shee̅ TSĚS-too.

374. **Can you show it to me on the road map?**
Můžete mi to ukázat na silniční mapě?
MOO-zhĕ-tĕmĭ taw OO-kah-zaht NAH-sĭl-nᵞĭch-nᵞee MAH-pyĕ?

375. **Can I avoid heavy traffic?**
Mohu se vyhnout rušnému provozu?
MAW-hoo-sĕ VĬ-hnoh‿oot ROOSH-neh-moo PRAW-vaw-zoo?

376. **May I park here [for a while]?**
Mohu zde [na chvíli] zaparkovat?
MAW-hoo zdĕ [NAH-khvee-lĭ] ZAH-pahr-kaw-vaht?

377. **May I park here overnight?**
Mohu zde parkovat přes noc?
MAW-hoo zdĕ PAHR-kaw-vaht PRZHĔS-nawts?

378. **Approach.**
Nájezd (na silnici).
NAH-yĕst (NAH-sĭl-nᵞĭ-tsĭ).

379. **Expressway.**
Dálnice.
DAHL-nᵞĭ-tsĕ.

380. **Fork.**
Rozvětvení (silnic).
RAWZ-vyĕt-vĕ-nᵞee (SIL-nᵞĭts).

381. **Garage.**
Opravna aut.
AW-prahv-nah ah˽oot.

382. **(Home) garage.**
Garáž.
GAH-rāhsh.

383. **Intersection.**
Křižovatka.
KRZHĬ-zhaw-vaht-kah.

384. **Major road.**
Hlavní silnice.
HLAHV-n^yee SĬL-n^yĭ-tsĕ.

385. **Parking lot.**
Parkoviště.
PAHR-kaw-vĭsh-t^yĕ.

386. **Traffic circle.**
Kruhový objezd.
KROO-haw-vēe AWB-yĕst.

387. **Traffic light.**
Dopravní světelný signál.
DAW-prahv-n^yee SVYĔ-tĕl-nee SĬG-nāhl.

See also "Road Signs," p. 221.

AUTO:
HELP ON THE ROAD
AUTO:
POMOC NA SILNICI

388. My car has broken down.
Mám porouchané auto.
mahm PAW-roh‿oo-khah-neh AH‿OO-taw.

389. Help me push [the car] to the side.
Pomozte mi odtlačit [auto] stranou.
*PAW-maws-tě mǐ AWT-tlah-chǐt [AH‿OO-
taw] STRAH-noh‿oo.*

390. Push me.
Zatlačte mi do auta.
ZAH-tlahch-tě mǐ DAW-ah‿oo-tah.

391. Lend me [a jack].
Půjčte mi [zdvihák].
POO‿YCH-tě mǐ [ZDVǏ-hahk].

392. Help me change the tire.
Pomozte mi vyměnit pneumatiku.
*PAW-maws-tě mǐ VǏ-mnʸě-nʸǐt PNĚ‿OO-mah-
tǐ-koo.*

393. My car is stuck [in the mud].
Auto mi uvázlo [v blátě].
AH‿OO-taw mǐ OO-vahz-law [VBLAH-tʸě].

394. — **in the ditch.** — v příkopu.
— *FPRZHEE-kaw-poo.*

395. **Drive me to the nearest gas station.**
Odvezte mě k nejbližší benzínové pumpě.
AWD-věs-tě mnᵘě KNAY-blĭsh-sheē BĔN-zee-naw-veh͞ POOM-pyě.

AUTO :
SERVICE STATION

AUTO :
ČERPACÍ STANICE A
OPRAVNA

396. **Give me [twenty] liters of [regular] premium gas.**
Dejte mi [dvacet] litrů [normálního] vyso-kooktanového benzínu.
DAY-tě mĭ [DVAH-tsĕt] LĬT-ro͞o [NAWR-mahl-nᵘee-haw] VĬ-saw-kaw-awk-tah-naw-veh͞-haw BĔN-zee͞-noo.

397. **Fill the gas tank.**
Naplňte mi nádrž.
NAH-půlnᵘ-tě mĭ NA͞H-důrsh.

398. **Change the oil.**
Vyměňte mi olej.
VĬ-mnᵘěnᵘ-tě mĭ AW-lay.

399. **Light, medium, heavy (oil).**
Lehký, střední, těžký (olej).
LĔKH-kee̅, STRZHĔD-nᵞee̅, TᵞĔSH-kee̅ (AW-lay).

400. **Put water in the radiator.**
Nalejte mi vodu do chladiče.
NAH-lay-tĕ mĭ VAW-doo DAW-khlah-dᵞĭ-chĕ.

401. **Recharge the battery.**
Nabijte mi baterii.
NAH-bee_y-tĕ mĭ BAH-tĕ-rĭ-yĭ.

402. **Lubricate the car.**
Promažte mi auto.
PRAW-mahsh-tĕ mĭ AH_OO-taw.

403. **Clean the windshield.**
Otřete mi ochranné sklo.
AW-trzhĕ-tĕ mĭ AW-khrahn-neh̅ sklaw.

404. **Could you wash it [now]?**
Mohl byste to [teď] umýt?
MAW-hŭl BĬS-tĕ taw [tĕtᵞ] OO-mee̅t?

405. **Adjust the brakes.**
Utáhněte mi brzdy.
OO-táh-hnᵞĕ-tĕ mĭ BŬRZ-dĭ.

406. **Check the tire pressure.**
Zkontrolujte tlak v pneumatikách.
SKAWN-traw-loo_y-tĕ tlahk FPNĔ_OO-mah-tĭ-kahkh.

407. Repair this tire.
Opravte tuto pneumatiku.
AW-prahf-tĕ TOO-taw PNĚ͜OO-mah-tĭ-koo.

408. The motor overheats.
Motor se přehřívá.
MAW-tawr-sĕ PRZHĚ-hrzhee-vah.

409. It makes a noise.
Dělá to hluk.
DᵛĚ-lah taw hlook.

410. The lights do not work.
Světla nefungují.
SVYĚT-lah NĚ-foon-goo-yee.

411. The car does not start.
Auto mi nechce zabrat.
AH͜OO-taw mĭ NĚ-khtsĕ ZAH-braht.

PARTS OF THE CAR AND AUTO EQUIPMENT
SOUČÁSTKY A VYBAVENÍ AUTA

412. Accelerator. Plynový pedál. *PLĬ-naw-vee PĚ-dahl.*

413. Air filter. Vzduchový filtr.
VZDOO-khaw-vee FĬL-tŭr.

414. Alcohol. Líh. *leekh.*

415. Antifreeze. Prostředek proti mrznutí vody.
PRAW-strzhě-děk PRAW-tʸĭ MŬRZ-noo-tʸee VAW-dĭ.

416. Axle. Osa. *AW-sah.*

417. Battery. Baterie. *BAH-tě-rĭ-yě.*

418. Bolt. Šroub. *shroh‿oop.*

419. Brakes. Brzdy. *BŬRZ-dĭ.*

420. Hand brake. Ruční brzda.
ROOCH-nʸee BŬRZ-dah.

421. Foot brake. Nožní brzda.
NAWZH-nʸee BŬRZ-dah.

422. Emergency brake. Záchranná brzda.
ZĀH-khrahn-nah BŬRZ-dah.

423. Bulb. Žárovka. *ZHĀH-rawf-kah.*

424. Bumper. Nárazník. *NĀH-rahz-nʸeek.*

425. Carburetor. Zplynovač. *SPLĬ-naw-vahch.*

426. Chains. Řetězy. *RZHĚ-tʸě-zĭ.*

427. Chassis. Podvozek auta.
PAWD-vaw-zěk AH‿OO-tah.

428. Choke (automatic).
(Automatická) škrticí klapka.
(AH‿OO-taw-mah-tĭts-kāh) SHKŬR-tʸĭ-tsee KLAHP-kah.

429. Clutch. Spojka. *SPOY-kah.*

430. Cylinder. Válec. *VĀH-lěts.*

431. **Differential.** Diferenciál. *DĬ-fĕ-rĕn-tsĭ-yahl.*

432. **Directional signal.** Ukazovatel směru.
OO-kah-zaw-vah-tĕl SMNᵘĔ-roo.

433. **Door.** Dveře. *DVE-rzhĕ.*

434. **Electrical system.** Elektrický systém.
Ĕ-lĕk-trĭts-kee SĬS-tehm.

435. **Engine.** Motor. *MAW-tawr.*

436. **Exhaust pipe.** Výfuková roura.
VĒE-foo-kaw-vah ROH‿OO-rah.

437. **Exterior.** Vnější část (OR: Zevnější).
VNᵘAY-shee chahst (OR: ZĔ-vnᵘay-shĕk).

438. **Fan.** Ventilátor. *VEN-tĭ-lah-tawr.*

439. **Fan belt.** Ventilátorový řemen.
VĔN-tĭ-lah-taw-raw-vee RZHĔ-mĕn.

440. **Fender.** Blatník. *BLAHT-nᵘeek.*

441. **Flashlight.**
Baterka (OR: Kapesní elektrická svítilna).
*BAH-tĕr-kah (OR: KAH-pĕs-nᵘee Ĕ-lĕk-trĭts-kah
SVĒE-tᵘĭl-nah).*

442. **Fuel pump.** Palivové čerpadlo.
PAH-lĭ-vaw-veh CHĔR-pahd-law.

443. **Fuse.** Pojistka. *PAW-yĭst-kah.*

444. **Gear shift.** Rychlostní páka.
RĬKH-lawst-nᵘee PĀH-kah.

445. **Generator.** Generátor. *GĔ-nĕ-rah-tawr.*

446. **Grease.** Mazadlo. *MAH-zahd-law.*

447. **Hammer.** Kladivo. *KLAH-dʸĭ-vaw.*

448. **Heater.** Topení. *TAW-pĕ-nʸee.*

449. **Hood.** Kapota. *KAH-paw-tah.*

450. **Horn.** Houkačka. *HOH‿OO-kahch-kah.*

451. **Horsepower.** Koňská síla.
KAWNʸ-skah̄ SEE-lah.

452. **Ignition.** Zapalování. *ZAH-pah-law-vah̄-nʸee.*

453. **Inner tube.** Duše (pneumatiky).
DOO-shĕ (PNĔ‿OO-mah-tĭ-kĭ).

454. **Instrument panel.** Přístrojová deska.
PRZHEE-straw-yaw-vah̄ DĔS-kah.

455. **Jack.** Zdihák. *ZDVĬ-hah̄k.*

456. **Key.** Klíč. *klēech.*

457. **License plate.** Tabulka s poznávací značkou.
TAH-bool-kah SPAW-znah̄-vah-tsee ZNAHCH-koh‿oo.

458. **Light.** Světlo. *SVYĔT-law.*

459. **Headlight.** Reflektor. *RĔ-flĕk-tawr.*

460. **Parking light.** Parkovací světlo.
PAHR-kaw-vah-tsee SVYĔT-law.

461. **Stop light.** Stopka. *STAWP-kah.*

462. **Taillight.** Zadní světlo.
   ZAHD-nᵞee SVYĚT-law.

463. **Lubrication system.** Mazací soustava.
   MAH-zah-tsee SOH_OO-stah-vah.

464. **Motor.** Motor. *MAW-tawr.*

465. **Muffler.** Tlumič výfuku.
   TLOO-mĭch VEE-foo-koo.

466. **Nail.** Hřebík. *HRZHĔ-beek.*

467. **Neutral gear.** Neutrál. *NĔ-oot-rahl.*

468. **Nut.** Matice. *MAH-tᵞĭ-tsĕ.*

469. **Oil.** Olej. *AW-lay.*

470. **Pedal.** Pedál. *PE-dahl.*

471. **Pliers** [LIT.: **Tongs for bending wire**].
   Kleště na ohýbání drátu.
   KLĔSH-tᵞĕ NAH-aw-hee-bah-nᵞee DRAH-too.

472. **Radiator.** Chladič. *KHLAH-dᵞĭch.*

473. **Radio.** Rádio. *RAH-dĭ-yaw.*

474. **Rags.** Hadry. *HAHD-rĭ.*

475. **Reverse gear.** Zpáteční rychlost.
   SPAH-tĕch-nᵞee RĬKH-lawst.

476. **Rope.** Lano. *LAH-naw.*

477. **Screw.** Šroubek. *SHROH_OO-bĕk.*

478. **Screwdriver.** Šroubovák.
   SHROH_OO-baw-vahk.

479. Shift. Přeřazování rychlostí.
PRZHĔ-rzhah-zaw-vāh-n^yēe RĬKH-laws-t^yee.

480. Automatic shift.
Automatické přeřazování rychlostí.
AH͜ OO-taw-mah-tĭts-keh PRZHĔ-rzhah-zaw-vah-n^yēe RĬKH-laws-t^yee.

481. Hand shift. Ruční přeřazování rychlostí.
ROOCH-n^yēe PRZHĔ-rzhah-zaw-vāh-n^yēe RĬKH-laws-t^yee.

482. Shock absorber. Tlumič nárazů.
TLOO-mĭch NĀH-rah-zoo.

483. Skid chains. Řetězy na kola.
RZHĔ-t^yĕ-zĭ NAH-kaw-lah.

484. Snow tires. Zimní pneumatiky.
ZĬM-n^yēe PNĔ͜ OO-mah-tĭ-kĭ.

485. Spark plugs. Svíčky. *SVĒECH-kĭ.*

486. Spring. Péro. *PĒH-raw.*

487. Starter. Spouštěč. *SPOH͜ OOSH-t^yĕch.*

488. Steering wheel. Volant. *VAW-lahnt.*

489. (Gas) tank. Nádrž (na benzín).
NĀH-dŭrsh (NAH-bĕn-zeen).

490. Tire. Pneumatika. *PNĔ͜ OO-mah-tĭ-kah.*

491. Spare tire. Náhradní pneumatika.
NĀH-hrahd-n^yēe PNĔ͜ OO-mah-tĭ-kah.

492. Tire pump. Pumpa na pneumatiky.
POOM-pah NAH-pnĕ͜ oo-mah-tĭ-kĭ.

493. Tools. Nářadí. *N$\overline{AH}$-rzhah-d$^y\overline{ee}$.*

494. Transmission. Rychlostní skříň.
R$\breve{I}$KH-lawst-n$^y\overline{ee}$ skrzheen^y.

495. Trunk. Kufr. *KOO-fŭr.*

496. Tube (inner tube). Duše (pneumatiky).
DOO-shĕ (PN$\breve{E}$_OO-mah-tĭ-kĭ).

497. Valve. Záklopka. *Z$\overline{AH}$-klawp-kah.*

498. Water cooling system. Chlazení vodou.
KHLAH-zĕ-n$^y\overline{ee}$ VAW-doh_oo.

499. Wheel. Kolo. *KAW-law.*

500. Front wheel. Přední kolo.
PRZH$\breve{E}$D-n$^y\overline{ee}$ KAW-law.

501. Rear wheel. Zadní kolo.
ZAHD-n$^y\overline{ee}$ KAW-law.

502. Windshield wiper. Stěrač. *ST$^y\breve{E}$-rahch.*

503. Wrench. Francouzský klíč.
FRAHN-tsoh_oo-skee k$\overline{lee}$ch.

MAIL
POŠTA

504. Where is [the post office]?
Kde je [pošta]?
gdĕ yĕ [PAWSH-tah]?

505. — a letter box. — poštovní schránka.
— *PAWSH-tawv-n^yee SKHRĀHN-kah.*

506. To which window should I go?
Ke které přepážce mám jít?
KĚ-ktě-reh PRZHĚ-pahsh-tsě mahm yeet?

507. I want to send this [by surface mail].
Toto chci poslat [obyčejnou poštou].
TAW-taw khtsї PAW-slaht [AW-bĭ-chay-noh‿oo PAWSH-toh‿oo].

508. — by air mail. — leteckou poštou.
— *LĚ-tĕts-koh‿oo PAWSH-toh‿oo.*

509. — special delivery. — jako spěšnou zásilku.
— *YAH-kaw SPYĚSH-noh‿oo ZĀH-sĭl-koo.*

510. — by registered mail. — doporučeně.
— *DAW-paw-roo-chě-n^yě.*

511. — by parcel post. — jako poštovní balík.
— *YAH-kaw PAWSH-tawv-n^yee BAH-leek.*

512. How much postage do I need?
Jaké je na to třeba poštovné?
YAH-keh yě NAH-taw TRZHĚ-bah PAWSH-tawv-neh?

513. The package contains [printed matter].
Tento balíček obsahuje [tiskoviny].
TĚN-taw BAH-lee-chěk AWP-sah-hoo-yě [T^yĬS-kaw-vĭ-nĭ].

514. — **fragile material.** — křehké zboží.
    — *KRZHĚKH-keh ZBAW-zhee.*

515. **I want to insure this [for 185 crowns (Kčs)].**
    Chci to pojistit [na sto osmdesát pět korun].
    khtsĭ taw PAW-yĭs-tyĭt [NAH-staw-aw-soom-dě-saht-pyĕt KAW-roon].

516. **Give me a receipt.**
    Dejte mi stvrzenku.
    DAY-tě mĭ STVŮR-zĕn-koo.

517. **Will it go out [today]?**
    Půjde to (ještě) [dnes]?
    POO͝_Y-dě taw (YĚSH-tyĕ) [dněs]?

518. **Give me two [60-heller] stamps.**
    Dejte mi dvě [šedesátihaléřové] známky.
    DAY-tě mĭ dvyĕ [SHĚ-dě-sah-tyĭ-hah-leh-rzhaw-veh] ZNAHM-kĭ.

519. **Where can I get a money order?**
    Kde mohu dostat peněžní poukázku?
    gdě MAW-hoo DAWS-taht PĚ-nyĕzh-nyee POH͝_OO-kahs-koo?

TELEGRAM
TELEGRAM

520. **I would like to send [a telegram].**
Chtěl bych poslat [telegram].
KHT^{y}ĚL-bĭkh PAW-slaht [TĚ-lĕ-grahm].

521. **— a night letter.** — noční telegram.
— NAWCH-n^{y}ēē TĚ-lĕ-grahm.

522. **— a cablegram.**
— kabelogram (OR: telegram).
— KAH-bĕ-law-grahm (OR: TĚ-lĕ-grahm).

523. **What is the rate per word?**
Jaká je sazba za jedno slovo?
YAH-kāh yĕ SAHZ-bah ZAH-yĕd-naw SLAW-vaw?

524. **What is the minimum charge?**
Jaká je minimální sazba?
YAH-kāh yĕ MĬ-nĭ-mahl-n^{y}ēē SAHZ-bah?

525. **When will an ordinary cablegram reach [London]?**
Za jak dlouho dojde obyčejný telegram (OR: kabelogram) [do Londýna]?
ZAH-yahk DLOH‿OO-haw DOY-dĕ AW-bĭ-chay-nēē TĚ-lĕ-grahm (OR: KAH-bĕ-law-grahm) [DAW-lawn-dēē-nah]?

TELEPHONE

TELEFON

526. **May I use the telephone?**
Mohu použít vašeho telefonu?
MAW-hoo PAW-oo-zheet VAH-shě-haw TĚ-lě-faw-noo?

527. **Will you dial this number for me?**
Vytočil byste mi toto číslo?
VĬ-taw-chĭl BĬS-tě mĭ TAW-taw CHEES-law?

528. **Operator, get me this number.**
Slečno, spojte mě s tímto číslem.
SLĚCH-naw, SPOY-tě mn^{y}ě STEEM-taw CHEES-lěm.

529. **Will you call me at this number?**
Zavolejte mi laskavě na toto číslo.
ZAH-vaw-lay-tě mi LAHS-kah-vyě NAH-taw-taw CHEES-law.

530. **My telephone number is [32-67-23].**
Moje telefonní číslo je [třicet dva, šedesát sedm, dvacet tři].
MAW-yě TĚ-lě-fawn-n^{y}ee CHEES-law yě [TRZHĬ-tsět dvah, SHĚ-de-saht SĚ-doom, DVAH-tsět trzhĭ].

531. **What is the charge for the first three minutes?**
Kolik je poplatek za první tři minuty?
KAW-lǐk yě PAW-plah-těk ZAH-pǔrv-nʸee trzhǐ MǏ-noo-tǐ?

532. **How much is a long-distance call [to Pardubice]?**
Kolik stojí dálkový rozhovor [do Pardubic]?
KAW-lǐk STAW-yee DĀHL-kaw-vee RAWZ-haw-vawr [DAW-pahr-doo-bǐts]?

533. **Hello (on the telephone).**
Haló!
HAH-law̄!

534. **They do not answer.**
Nikdo se nehlásí.
NʸǏ-gdaw-sě NĚ-hlāh-see.

535. **The line is busy.**
Linka je obsazena.
LǏN-kah yě AWP-sah-zě-nah.

536. **Sorry, wrong number.**
Promiňte, vytočil jste nesprávné číslo.
PRAW-mǐnʸ-tě, VǏ-taw-chǐl-stě NĚ-sprahv-neh CHĒ̄ES-law.

537. **This is [John Taylor] speaking.**
U telefonu je [John Taylor].
OO-tě-lě-faw-noo yě [dzhawn TAY-lawr].

538. **Whom do you want to speak to?**
S kým chcete mluvit?
skeem KHTSĚ-tě MLOO-vĭt?

539. **Hold the line.**
Zůstaňte u telefonu.
ZOO-stanʸ-tě OO-tě-lě-faw-noo.

540. **Dial (the number) again.**
Vytočte to (číslo) ještě jednou.
VĬ-tawch-tě taw (CHEES-law) YĚSH-tʸě YĚD-noh‿oo.

541. **The connection is poor.**
Je špatné spojení.
yě SHPAHT-neh SPAW-yě-nʸee.

542. **Speak louder.**
Mluvte hlasitěji!
MLOOF-tě HLAH-sĭ-tʸě-yĭ!

543. **He is not here.**
Není tady.
NE-nʸee TAH-dĭ.

544. **May I leave a message?**
Mohl bych nechat vzkaz?
MAW-hŭl-bĭkh NĚ-khaht fskahs?

545. **Call me back.**
Zavolejte mi zpátky.
ZAH-vaw-lay-tě mĭ SPAH T-kĭ.

546. I will call back later.

Zavolám vám znovu později.

ZAH-vaw-la̅hm va̅hm ZNAW-voo PAWZ-dᵘĕ-yĭ.

547. I will wait for your call [until five o'clock].

Budu čekat [až do pěti], že mi zavoláte.

BOO-doo CHĚ-kaht [azh DAW-pyĕ-tᵘĭ], zhĕ mĭ ZAH-vaw-la̅h-tĕ.

548. You are wanted on the telephone.

Jděte k telefonu; někdo chce s vámi mluvit.

YDᵘĚ-tĕ KTĚ-lĕ-faw-noo; NᵘĚ-gdaw khtsĕ SVA̅H-mi MLOO-vĭt.

See also "Making Yourself Understood," p. 27.

HOTEL
HOTEL

549. I am looking for a good hotel.

Hledám nějaký dobrý hotel.

HLĚ-da̅hm NᵘĚ-yah-kee DAWB-ree HAW-tĕl.

550. What is the best hotel here?

Který je zde nejlepší hotel?

KTĚ-re̅e yĕ zdĕ NAY-lĕp-she̅e HAW-tĕl?

551. I am looking for [an inexpensive hotel].

Hledám [nějaký levný hotel].

HLĚ-da̅hm [NᵘĚ-yah-ke̅e LĚV-nee HAW-tĕl].

552. — a boarding house (OR: pension).
    — byt se stravou* (OR: penzión).
    — bǐt SĚ-strah-voh‿oo (OR: PĚN-zǐ-yāwn).

553. I want to be in the center of town.
    Chci bydlet ve středu města.
    khtsǐ BǏD-lět VĚ-strzhě-doo MNʸĚS-tah.

554. I want a quiet location.
    Chci tiché prostředí.
    khtsǐ TʸǏ-kheh PRAW-strzhě-dʸee.

555. I prefer to be close to [the University].
    Rád bych bydlel blízko [university].
    RĀHD-bǐkh BǏD-lěl BLEES-kaw [OO-nǐ-věr-
    zǐ-tǐ].

556. I have a reservation for tonight.
    Mám zamluvený nocleh na dnešek.
    māhm ZAH-mloo-vě-nee NAWTS-lěkh NAH-
    dně-shěk.

557. Where is the registration desk?
    Kde je zde příjem hostů?
    gdě yě zdě PRZHEE-yěm HAWS-too?

558. Fill out this registration form.
    Vyplňte tento formulář.
    VǏ-půlnʸ-tě TĚN-taw FAWR-moo-lāhrzh.

* The literal meaning of byt se stravou is "lodging with food."

559. Write your signature here.
Zde se podepište.
ZDĚ-sě PAW-dě-přish-tě.

560. Leave your passport.
Nechte tu svůj pas.
NĚKH-tě too svoo͡_y pahs.

561. Pick it up later.
Vyzvedněte si jej později.
VĬ-zvěd-nʸě-tě-sĭ yay PAWZ-dʸě-yĭ.

562. Do you have [a single room]?
Máte volný [jednolůžkový pokoj]?
MAH-tě VAWL-nee [YĚD-naw-loosh-kaw-vee PAW-koy]?

563. — a double room. — dvojlůžkový pokoj.
— *DVOY-loosh-kaw-vee PAW-koy.*

564. — an air-conditioned room.
— pokoj s umělým chlazením.
— *PAW-koy SOO-mnʸě-leem KHLAH-zě-nʸeem.*

565. — a quiet room. — tichý pokoj.
— *TʸĬ-khee PAW-koy.*

566. — a cheerful room. — světlý pokoj.
— *SVYĚT-lee PAW-koy.*

567. — a room with windows on the street.
— pokoj s okny do ulice.
— *PAW-koy SAWK-nĭ DAW-oo-lĭ-tsě.*

568. **— a room with windows on the court.**
  — pokoj s okny do dvora.
  — *PAW-koy SAWK-nĭ DAW-dvaw-rah.*

569. **Do you have a suite?**
  Máte volné apartmá?
  MĀH-tĕ VAWL-neh AH-pahrt-mah?

570. **I want a room [with a double bed].**
  Chtěl bych pokoj [s dvojitou postelí].
  KHT^yĔL-bĭkh PAW-koy [ZDVAW-yĭ-toh_oo
  PAW-stĕ-lee].

571. **— with twin beds.**
  — se dvěma jednoduchými postelemi.
  — *SE-dvyĕ-mah YĔD-naw-doo-khee-mĭ PAW-*
  stĕ-lĕ-mĭ.

572. **— with a bath.** — s koupelnou.
  — *SKOH_OO-pĕl-noh_oo.*

573. **— with a shower.** — se sprchou.
  — *SE-spŭr-khoh_oo.*

574. **— with running water.** — s tekoucí vodou.
  — *STĔ-koh_oo-tsee VAW-dohoo.*

575. **— with hot water.** — s teplou vodou.
  — *STĔP-loh_oo VAW-doh_oo.*

576. **— with a balcony.** — s balkónem.
  — *ZBAHL-kaw-něm.*

577. **— with a radio.** — s rádiem.
  — *SRĀH-dĭ-yěm.*

578. — **with a telephone.** — s telefonem.
     — *STĚ-lĕ-faw-něm.*

579. — **with television.** — s televizí.
     — *STĚ-lĕ-vĭ-zee.*

580. **I shall take a room [for one night].**
Vezmu si u vás pokoj [na jednu noc].
*VEZ-moo-sĭ OO-vahs PAW-koy [NAH-yĕd-noo
nawts].*

581. — **for several days.** — na několik dnů.
     —*NAH-nʸĕ-kaw-lĭk dnoo.*

582. — **for a week or so.** — přibližně na týden.
     — *PRZHĬ-blĭzh-nʸě NAH-tee-děn.*

583. — **for two persons.** — pro dvě osoby.
     — *PRAW-dvyě AW-saw-bĭ.*

584. **Can I have it [with meals]?**
Mohu to mít [se stravou]?
MAW-hoo taw meet [SĚ-strah-voh‿oo]?

585. — **without meals.** — bez stravy.
     — *BĚS-strah-vĭ.*

586. — **with breakfast only.**
     — pouze se snídaní.
     — *POH‿OO-zě SĚ-snʸee-dah-nʸee.*

587. **What is the rate [per day]?**
Kolik stojí pokoj [denně]?
KAW-lik STAW-yee PAW-koy [DĚN-nʸě]?

588. — **per week.** — týdenně.
— $\overline{TEE}$-děn-n^{y}ě.

589. — **per month.** — měsíčně.
— $MN^y\breve{E}$-$\overline{seech}$-n^{y}ě.

590. **Are tax and service included?**
Zahrnuje cena daň a služby?
ZAH-hŭr-noo-yě TS$\breve{E}$-nah dahn^y ah SLOOZH-bǐ?

591. **I would like to see the room.**
Rád bych viděl ten pokoj.
$\overline{RAHD}$-bǐkh V$\check{I}$-d^{y}ěl těn PAW-koy.

592. **Have you something [better]?**
Máte něco [lepšího]?
$\overline{MAH}$-tě N$^y\breve{E}$-tsaw [L$\breve{E}$P-$\overline{shee}$-haw]?

593. — **cheaper.** — levnějšího.
— $L\breve{E}V$-n^{y}ay-$\overline{shee}$-haw.

594. — **larger.** — většího. — $VY\breve{E}T$-$\overline{shee}$-haw.

595. — **smaller.** — menšího. — $M\breve{E}N$-$\overline{shee}$-haw.

596. — **[on a lower] on a higher floor.**
— [v nižším] ve vyšším poschodí.
— [$VN^y\check{I}SH$-$\overline{sheem}$] V$\breve{E}$-vǐsh-$\overline{sheem}$ PAW-skhaw-d$^y\overline{ee}$.

597. — **with more light.** — světlejšího.
SVY$\breve{E}T$-lay-$\overline{shee}$-haw.

598. — **with more air.** — vzdušnějšího.
— *VZDOOSH-nʸay-shĕe-haw.*

599. — **more attractively furnished.**
— vkusněji zařízeného.
— *FKOOS-nʸĕ-yĭ ZAH-rzhĕe-zĕ-nĕh-haw.*

600. — **with a better view.**
— s lepší vyhlídkou.
— *SLĔP-shĕe VĬ-hlĕet-koh_oo.*

601. **This room is too noisy.**
Tento pokoj je příliš hlučný.
*TĔN-taw PAW-koy yĕ PRZHĔE-lĭsh
HLOOCH-nĕe.*

602. **This suits me.**
Toto mi vyhovuje.
TAW-taw mĭ VĬ-haw-voo-yĕ.

603. **Is there an elevator?**
Je tu výtah?
yĕ too VĔE-takh?

604. **Upstairs.**
Nahoru.
NAH-haw-roo.

605. **Downstairs.**
Dolů.
DAW-loo.

606. **What is my room number?**
Jaké číslo má můj pokoj?
YAH-keh CHEES-law mah moo͟_y PAW-koy?

607. **Give me my room key.**
Dejte mi klíč od pokoje.
DAY-tě mǐ kleech AWT-paw-kaw-yě.

608. **Wake me [at eight in the morning].**
Vzbuďte mě [v osm hodin ráno].
VZBOOTʸ-tě mnʸě [VAW-soom HAW-dʸǐn
RAH-naw].

609. **Do not disturb me until nine o'clock.**
Do devíti hodin mě nerušte.
DAW-dě-vee-tʸǐ HAW-dʸǐn mnʸě NĚ-roosh-tě.

610. **I want [breakfast] in my room.**
Chci [snídat] ve svém pokoji.
khtsǐ [SNʸEE-daht] VE-svehm PAW-kaw-yǐ.

611. **Room service, please.**
Spojte mě s pokojovou službou.
SPOY-tě mnʸě SPAW-kaw-yaw-voh͟_oo
SLOOZH-boh͟_oo.

612. **I want to speak [to the manager].**
Chci mluvit [s ředitelem].
khtsǐ MLOO-vǐt [SRZHĚ-dʸǐ-tě-lěm].

613. **Have you [a letter] for me?**
Máte tu pro mne [dopis]?
MAH-te too PRAW-mně [DAW-pǐs]?

614. — a message. — vzkaz. — *fskahs.*

615. — a parcel. — balík. — *BAH-leek.*

616. Send [a chambermaid].
Pošlete mi [pokojskou].
PAW-shlě-tě mi [PAW-koy-skoh‿oo].

617. — a valet. — sluhu. — *SLOO-hoo.*

618. — a bellhop (OR: messenger).
— poslíčka. — *PAW-sleech-kah.*

619. a waiter. — číšníka.
— *CHEEESH-nʸee-kah.*

620. — a porter. — nosiče. — *NAW-sĭ-chě.*

621. I am expecting [a friend].
Očekávám [přítele].
AW-chě-kāh-vahm [PRZHEE-tě-lě].

622. — a telephone call. — telefonní rozhovor.
— *TĚ-lě-fawn-nʸee RAWZ-haw-vawr.*

623. Spray (it) for [insects].
Postříkejte to proti [hmyzu].
PAW-strzhee-kay-tě taw PRAW-tʸĭ [HMĬ-zoo].

624. — vermin. — havěti. — *HAH-vyě-tʸĭ.*

625. May I leave [these valuables] in the hotel safe?

Mohu si uložit [tyto cennosti] v hotelovém trezoru?

MAW-hoo-sĭ OO-law-zhĭt [TĬ-taw TSĔN-naws-tᵞĭ] VHAW-tĕ-law-vēhm TRĔ-zaw-roo?

626. I would like to get my [things] from the safe.

Chtěl bych si vyzvednout své [věci] z trezoru.

KHTᵞĔL-bĭkh-sĭ VĬ-zvĕd-noh‿oot svēh [VYĔ-tsĭ] STRĔ-zaw-roo.

627. When must I check out (LIT.: When is the time of departure from the hotel)?

Kdy je doba odchodu z hotelu?

gdĭ yĕ DAW-bah AWT-khaw-doo SKHAW-tĕ-loo?

628. I am leaving [at ten o'clock].

Odjíždím [v deset hodin].

AWD-yēezh-dᵞeem [VDĔ-sĕt HAW-dᵞĭn].

629. Make out my bill [as soon as possible].

Připravte mi účet [co nejdříve].

PRZHĬ-prahf-tĕ mĭ OO-chĕt [tsaw NAY-drzhee-vĕ].

630. Forward my mail [to Marienbad].
Došlete mi poštu [do Mariánských Lázní].
DAW-shlĕ-tĕ mĭ PAWSH-too [DAW-mah-řĭ-
yāhn-skeekh LĀHZ-n^{y}ēe].

631. The cashier.
Pokladní.
PAW-klahd-n^{y}ēe.

632. The doorman.
Vrátný.
VRĀHT-nēe.

633. The lobby.
Hala.
HAH-lah.

634. The roof.
Střecha.
STRZHĔ-khah.

635. The room clerk.
Recepční úředník.
RĔ-tsĕp-chn^{y}ēe ŌŌ-rzhĕd-n^{y}eek.

CHAMBERMAID
POKOJSKÁ

636. The door doesn't lock.
Dveře se nedají zamknout.
DVĔ-rzhĕ-sĕ NĔ-dah-yēe ZAHMK-noh‿oot.

637. The [toilet] is broken.
[Záchod] nefunguje.
[ZĀH-khawt] NĚ-foon-goo-yě.

638. The room is too [cold] hot.
V pokoji je příliš [chladno] teplo.
FPAW-kaw-yǐ yě PRZHĒE-lǐsh [KHLAHD-naw] TĚP-law.

639. There is no hot water.
Neteče horká voda.
NĚ-tě-chě HAWR-kāh VAW-dah.

640. Wash and iron [this shirt].
Vyperte a vyžehlete mi [tuto košili].
VǏ-pěr-tě ah VǏ-zhě-hlě-tě mǐ [TOO-taw KAW-shǐ-lǐ].

641. Dry-clean and press [this suit].
Dejte mi vyčistit a vyžehlit [tento oblek].
DAY-tě mǐ VǏ-chǐs-t^yǐt ah VǏ-zhě-hlǐt [TĚN-taw AWB-lěk].

642. Bring me [another blanket].
Přineste mi [ještě jednu pokrývku].
PRZHǏ-něs-tě mǐ [YĚSH-t^yě YED-noo PAW-krēef-koo].

643. — a bath mat. — předložku do koupelny.
— PRZHĚD-lawsh-koo DAW-koh‿oo-pěl-nǐ.

644. — a bed sheet. — prostěradlo.
— PRAW-st^yě-rahd-law.

645. — **coathangers.** — ramínka na šaty.
— *RAH-mēen-kah NAH-shah-tĭ.*

646. — **a glass.** — sklenici. — *SKLĚ-nʸĭ-tsĭ.*

647. — **a pillow.** — polštář. — *PAWLSH-tāhrzh.*

648. — **a pillowcase.** — povlak na polštář.
— *PAW-vlahk NAH-pawlsh-tāhrzh.*

649. — **some soap.** — kousek mýdla.
— *KOH‿OO-sĕk MĒĒD-lah.*

650. — **toilet paper.** — toaletní papír.
— *TAW-ah-lĕt-nʸee PAH-pēer.*

651. — **a towel.** — ručník. — *ROOCH-nʸeek.*

652. **Change the sheets.**
Vyměňte mi povlaky.
VĬ-mnʸĕnʸ-tĕ mĭ PAW-vlah-kĭ.

653. **Make the bed.**
Ustelte mi postel.
OO-stĕl-tĕ mĭ PAW-stĕl.

654. **Come back later.**
Vraťte se později.
VRAHTʸ-tĕ-sĕ PAWZ-dʸĕ-yĭ.

RENTING AN APARTMENT
PRONAJÍMÁNÍ BYTU

**655. I want to rent [a furnished] an un-
furnished apartment.**
Chci si pronajmout [zařízený] nezařízený
byt.
*KHTSĪ-sĭ PRAW-nah‿y-moh‿oot [ZAH-rzhee-
zě-nee] NĚ-zah-rzhee-zě-nee bĭt.*

656. With a bathroom.
S koupelnou.
SKOH‿OO-pěl-noh‿oo.

657. With two bedrooms.
Se dvěma ložnicemi.
SĚ-dvyě-mah LAWZH-nʸĭ-tsě-mĭ.

658. With a living room.
S obývacím pokojem.
SAW-bee-vah-tseem PAW-kaw-yěm.

659. With a dining room.
S jídelnou.
SYĒĒ-děl-noh‿oo.

660. With a kitchen.
S kuchyní.
SKOO-khĭ-nʸee.

661. Do you furnish (LIT: **give the tenants**)
[the linen]?
Dáváte nájemníkům [ložní prádlo]?
$D\overline{AH}$-vah-tĕ $N\overline{AH}$-yĕm-n^{y}ee-koom [LAWZH-
n^{y}ee PR$\overline{AH}$D-law]?

662. — the dishes. — nádobí. — $N\overline{AH}$-daw-bee.

663. Do you furnish maid service (LIT: **Will**
someone go to the apartment to do the
chores)?
Bude (do bytu) chodit někdo uklízet?
BOO-dĕ (DAW-bĭ-too) KHAW-d^{y}ĭt N^{y}Ĕ-gdaw
OO-klee-zĕt?

664. Must I sign a lease?
Musím podepsat smlouvu?
MOO-seem PAW-dĕ-psaht SMLOH‿OO-voo?

APARTMENT: USEFUL WORDS

BYT: UŽITEČNÉ VÝRAZY

665. Alarm clock. Budík. BOO-d$^y\overline{ee}$k.

666. Ash-tray. Popelníček. PAW-pĕl-n^{y}ee-chĕk.

667. Baby carriage. Kočárek. KAW-chah-rĕk.

668. **Baby sitter.** Hlídačka dětí.
HLĒĒ-dahch-kah DʸĔ-tʸēē.

669. **Bottle opener.** Otvírač lahví.
AWT-vēē-rahch LAH-hvēē.

670. **Broom.** Koště. *KAWSH-tʸĕ.*

671. **Can opener.** Otvírač konzerv.
AWT-vēē-rahch KAWN-zĕrf.

672. **Cat.** Kočka. *KAWCH-kah.*

673. **Chair.** Židle. *ZHĬD-lĕ.*

674. **Chest of drawers.** Prádelník. *PRĀH-dĕl-nʸēēk.*

675. **Clock.** Hodiny. *HAW-dʸĭ-nĭ.*

676. **Closet.** Šatník. *SHAHT-nʸēēk.*

677. **Cook.** Kuchař (FEMININE: Kuchařka).
KOO-khahrzh (KOO-khahrz-kah).

678. **Cork.** Zátka. *ZĀHT-kah.*

679. **Corkscrew.** Vývrtka. *VĒĒ-vŭrt-kah.*

680. **Crib.** Dětská postýlka.
DʸĔTS-kāh PAW-stēēl-kah.

681. **Cushion.** Poduška. *PAW-doosh-kah.*

682. **Dishwasher.** Stroj na umývání nádobí.
stroy NAH-oo-mēē-vāh-nʸēē NĀH-daw-bēē.

683. **Dog.** Pes. *pĕs.*

684. **Drapes.** Záclony. *ZAH-tslaw-nĭ.*

685. Dryer. Stroj na sušení prádla (OR: Sušírna).
   stroy NAH-soo-shĕ-nʸēē PRĀHD-lah (OR: *SOO-sheer-nah*).

686. Fan. Ventilátor. *VĔN-tĭ-lāh-tawr.*

687. Hassock. Stolička. *STAW-lĭch-kah.*

688. Housemaid. Služebná. *SLOO-zhĕb-nāh.*

689. Lamp. Lampa. *LAHM-pah.*

690. Light bulb. Žárovka. *ZHĀH-rawf-kah.*

691. Linens. Prádlo. *PRĀHD-law.*

692. Mirror. Zrcadlo. *ZŬR-tsahd-law.*

693. Mosquito net. Sít' proti komárům.
   sēetʸ PRAW-tʸĭ KAW-mah-room.

694. Napkins. Ubrousky. *OO-broh‿oos-kĭ.*

695. Pail. Kbelík. *GBĔ-lēek.*

696. Rug. Koberec. *KAW-bĕ-rĕts.*

697. Sink. Dřez. *drzhĕs.*

698. Stopper. Zátka. *ZĀHT-kah.*

699. Table. Stůl. *stōol.*

700. Tablecloth. Ubrus. *OO-broos.*

701. Tray. Podnos. *PAWD-naws.*

702. Vase. Váza. *VĀH-zah.*

703. Venetian blinds. Žaluzie. *ZHAH-loo-zĭ-yĕ.*

704. Washing machine. Pračka. *PRAHCH-kah.*

705. **Whiskbroom.** Smetáček. *SMĚ-tah-chĕk.*

706. **Window shades.** Rolety. *RAW-lĕ-tĭ.*

CAFÉ AND BAR
KAVÁRNA A BAR

707. **[Bartender,] I'd like [a drink].**
[Pane vrchní,] chtěl bych [něco k pití].
[PAH-ně VŬRKH-nᵞee,] KHTᵞĚL-bĭkh [Nᵞ Ě-tsaw KPĬ-tᵞee].

708. **— a cocktail.** — koktejl. — *KAWK-tayl.*

709. **— a bottle of mineral water [with gas] without gas.**
— láhev [šumivé] nešumivé minerálky.
— *LĀH-hĕf [SHOO-mĭ-veh] NE-shoo-mĭ-veh MĬ-ně-rahl-kĭ.*

710. **— a non-alcoholic drink.**
— nealkoholický nápoj.
— *NĚ-ahl-kaw-haw-lĭts-kee NĀH-poy.*

711. **— a bottled fruit drink.**
— ovocný nápoj v láhvi.
— *AW-vawts-nee NĀH-poy VLĀH-hvĭ.*

712. **— a lemonade.** — limonádu.
— *LĬ-maw-nah-doo.*

713. — **a whiskey [and soda].**
   — whisky [se sodou].
   — *VĬS-kĭ [SĚ-saw-doh‿oo].*

714. — **a cognac.** — koňak. — *KAW-nʸahk.*

715. — **a liqueur.** — likér. — *LI-kēhr.*

716. — **a [light] dark beer.**
   — [světlé] černé pivo.
   — *[SVYĚT-lēh] CHĔR-neh PĬ-vaw.*

717. — **a glass of sherry.** — sklenici sherry.
   — *SKLĚ-nʸĭ-tsĭ SHĔ-rĭ.*

718. — **champagne.** — šampaňské.
   — *SHAHM-pahnʸ-skēh.*

719. — **[red] white wine.**
   — [červené] bílé víno.
   — *[CHĔR-vě-nēh] BĒE-lēh VĒE-naw.*

720. **Let's have another.**
   Dejme si ještě jednu.
   DAY-mě-sĭ YĚSH-tʸě YĚD-noo.

721. **To your health.**
   Na (vaše) zdraví!
   NAH-(vah-shě) ZDRAH-vēe!

RESTAURANT
RESTAURACE

722. Can you recommend a typical restaurant [for dinner]?

Můžete mi doporučit rázovitou restauraci [kde podávají dobré obědy]?

MŌO-zhě-tě mǐ DAW-paw-roo-chǐt RĀH-zaw-vǐ-toh͝_oo RĔS-tah͝_oo-rah-tsǐ [gdě PAW-dah-vah-yee DAWB-reh AW-byě-dǐ]?

723. — for breakfast.

— kde podávají dobré snídaně.

— gdě PAW-dah-vah-yee DAWB-reh SN^yEE-dah-n^yě.

724. — for lunch.

— kde podávají dobré polední svačiny.

— gdě PAW-dah-vah-yee DAWB-reh PAW-lěd-n^yee SVAH-chǐ-nǐ.

725. — for a sandwich.

— kde podávají dobré obložené chlebíčky.

— gdě PAW-dah-vah-yee DAWB-reh AWB-law-zhě-neh KHLĔ-beech-kǐ.

726. At what time is [supper] served?

V kolik hodin se podává [večeře]?

FKAW-lǐk HAW-d^yǐn-sě PAW-dah-vah [VĔ-chě-rzhě]?

727. **Are you my waiter** (OR: **waitress**) (LIT: **Do you serve at my table**)?
Obsluhujete u mého stolu?
AWP-sloo-hoo-yě-tě OO-meh-haw STAW-loo?

728. **Are you my wine steward** (LIT: **Can I order wine from you**)?
Mohu u vás objednat víno?
MAW-hoo OO-vahs AWB-yěd-naht VEE-naw?

729. **Give me a table [by the window], if possible.**
Dejte mi stůl [u okna], jestli můžete.
DAY-tě mǐ stool [OO-awk-nah], YĚST-lǐ MOO-zhe-te.

730. — **in the corner.** — v rohu. — *VRAW-hoo.*

731. — **outdoors.** — venku. — *VĚN-koo.*

732. — **indoors.** — vevnitř. — *VĚ-vnʸǐtrzh.*

733. **We want to dine à la carte.**
Vybereme si jednotlivá jídla.
VǏ-bě-ře-mě-sǐ YĚD-nawt-lǐ-vah YEED-lah.

734. **We want to dine table d'hôte.**
Objednáme si kompletní obědy.
AWB-yěd-nah-mě-sǐ KAWM-plět-nʸee AW-byě-dǐ.

735. **What is the specialty of the house?**
Co je vaše specialita?
tsaw yě VAH-shě SPE-tsǐ-yah-lǐ-tah?

736. **What kind of [fish] do you have today?**
Jaké dnes podáváte [ryby]?
YAH-keh dněs PAW-dah-vah-te [RĬ-bĭ]?

737. **Please serve us as quickly as you can.**
Obslužte nás laskavě co možná nejdříve.
AWP-sloosh-tě nahs LAHS-kah-vyě tsaw MAWZH-nah NAY-drzhee-vě.

738. **Bring me [the menu].**
Přineste mi [jídelní lístek].
PRZHĬ-něs-tě mĭ [YEE-děl-nʸee LEES-těk].

739. **— the wine list.** — ceník vín.
— TSĚ-nʸeek veen.

740. **— a napkin.** — ubrousek. — *OOB-roh‿oo-sěk.*

741. **— bread.** — chleba. — *KHLĚ-bah.*

742. **— butter.** — máslo. — *MAHS-law.*

743. **— a cup.** — šálek. — *SHAH-lěk.*

744. **— a fork.** — vidličku. — *VĬD-lĭch-koo.*

745. **— a glass.** — skleničku. — *SKLĚ-nʸĭch-koo.*

746. **— a [sharp] knife.** — [ostrý] nůž.
— [AWST-ree] noosh.

747. **— a plate.** — talíř. — *TAH-leerzh.*

748. **— a soup spoon.** — polévkovou lžíci.
— PAW-lehf-kaw-voh‿oo LZHEE-tsĭ.

749. — **a teaspoon** (LIT: **coffee spoon**).
— kávovou lžičku.
— *KAH-vaw-voh_oo LZHĬCH-koo.*

750. **I want something plain.**
Chci něco obyčejného (OR: prostého).
khtsĭ NʸĔ-tsaw AW-bĭ-chay-neh-haw (OR:
PRAWS-teh-haw).

751. **Is it [canned]?**
Je to [z konzervy]?
yĕ taw [SKAWN-zĕr-vĭ]?

752. — **fatty.** — tučné. — *TOOCH-neh.*

753. — **fresh.** — čerstvé. — *CHĔRST-veh.*

754. — **frozen.** — zmražené — *ZMRAH-zhĕ-neh.*

755. — **greasy.** — mastné. — *MAHST-neh.*

756. — **lean.** — libové. — *LĬ-baw-veh.*

757. — **peppery.** — ostré. — *AWST-reh.*

758. — **[very] salty.** — [velmi] slané.
— [*VĔL-mĭ*] *SLAH-neh.*

759. — **spicy.** — kořeněné. — *KAW-rzhĕ-nʸĕ-neh.*

760. — **[very] sweet.** — [velmi] sladké.
— [*VĔL-mĭ*] *SLAHT-keh.*

761. **How is it prepared?**
Jak je to připravované?
yahk yĕ taw PRZĬ-prah-vaw-vah-neh?

762. **Is it [baked]?**
Je to [pečené]?
yě taw [PĚ-chě-neh]?

763. — **boiled.** — vařené. — *VAH-rzhě-neh.*

764. — **breaded.** — obalované v housce.
— *AW-bah-law-vah-neh VHOH‿OOS-tsě.*

765. — **chopped.** — sekané. — *SĚ-kah-neh.*

766. — **fried.** — smažené. — *SMAH-zhě-neh.*

767. — **grilled.** — pečené na rožni.
— *PĚ-chě-neh NAH-rawzh-nⁱ̌.*

768. — **poached.** — sazené v mléku.
— *SAH-zě-neh VMLEH-koo.*

769. — **roasted.** — pečené. — *PĚ-chě-neh.*

770. — **sautéed.** — dušené. — *DOO-shě-neh.*

771. — **on a skewer.** — na špejli.
— *NAH-shpay-lǐ.*

772. **This is [stale].**
Toto je [okoralé].
TAW-taw yě [AW-kaw-rah-leh].

773. — **too tough.** — příliš tvrdé.
— *PRZHEE-lǐsh TVŬR-deh.*

774. — **too dry.** — příliš vysušené.
— *PRZHEE-lǐsh VǏ-soo-shě-neh.*

775. **I like the meat [rare].**
Chci to maso [do krvava].
khtsĭ taw MAH-saw [DAW-kŭr-vah-vah].

776. **— medium.** — ne moc vypečené.
— ně mawts VĬ-pě-chě-neh.

777. **— well done.** — hodně vypečené.
— HAWD-nʸě VĬ-pě-chě-neh.

778. **The dish is [undercooked].**
Toto jídlo je [nedovařené].
*TAW-taw YEED-law yě [NĚ-daw-vah-rzhě-
neh].*

779. **— burned.** — připálené.
— PRZHĬ-pah-lě-neh.

780. **Does it taste like [cod]?**
Chutná to jako [treska]?
KHOOT-nah taw YAH-kaw [TRĚS-kah]?

781. **A little more.**
Ještě trochu.
YĚSH-tʸě TRAW-khoo.

782. **A little less.**
Trochu méně.
TRAW-khoo MĒH-nʸě.

783. **A small portion.**
Malou porci.
MAH-loh‿oo PAWR-tsĭ.

784. Enough.
Stačí.
STAH-chee.

785. This is not clean.
Toto není čisté.
TAW-taw NĚ-nʸee CHĬS-teh.

786. This is too cold.
Toto je příliš studené.
TAW-taw yě PRZHEE-lĭsh STOO-dě-neh.

787. I did not order this.
Toto jsem neobjednal.
TAW-toy-sěm NĚ-awb-yěd-nahl.

788. You may take this away.
Toto můžete odnést.
TAW-taw MOO-zhě-tě AWD-nehst.

789. May I change this for [a salad]?
Mohu si namísto tohoto vzít [salát]?
MAW-hoo-sǐ NAH-mees-taw TAW-haw-taw vzeet [SAH-laht]?

790. What flavors do you have?
Jaké příchuti si mohu vybrat?
YAH-keh PRZHEE-khoo-tʸĭ-sǐ MAW-hoo VĬ-braht?

791. The check, please.
Pane vrchní,* prosím účet.
PAH-ně VŬRKH-nʸee̅, PRAW-see̅m O̅O̅-chět.

792. Is the tip included?
Je v tom zahrnuto spropitné?
yě ftawm ZAH-hŭr-noo-taw SPRAW-pĭt-ne̅h?

793. There is a mistake in the bill.
V účtě je chyba.
VO̅O̅CH-tʸě yě KHĬ-bah.

794. What are these charges for?
Zač mi účtujete tohleto?
zahch mĭ O̅O̅CH-too-yě-tě TAW-hlě-taw?

795. Keep the change.
Zbytek si nechte.
ZBĬ-těk-sĭ NĚKH-tě.

796. The food and service were excellent.
Jídlo i obsluha byla skvělá.
YEE̅D-law i AWP-sloo-hah BĬ-lah SKVYĚ-la̅h.

797. Hearty appetite!
Dobré chutnání!
DAWB-re̅h KHOO̅T-nah-nʸee̅!

---

* *Pane vrchní* is the form of address referring to a male waiter. A waitress should be addressed as *slečno* (pronounced *SLĚCH-naw*).

FOOD : SEASONINGS
JÍDLA : KOŘENÍ

798. **Catsup.** Kečup. *KĚ-choop.*

799. **Condiments.** Koření. *KAW-rzhĕ-nᵞee.*

800. **Garlic.** Česnek. *CHĚS-nĕk.*

801. **Mayonnaise.** Majonéza. *MAH-yaw-nēh-zah.*

802. **[Hot] mustard.** [Ostrá] hořčice.
[*AWST-rah*] *HAWRSH-chĭ-tsĕ.*

803. **Oil.** Olej. *AW-lay.*

804. **Pepper.** Pepř. *pĕprzh.*

805. **Salt.** Sůl. *sool.*

806. **Sauce.** Omáčka. *AW-māhch-kah.*

807. **Sugar.** Cukr. *TSOO-kŭr.*

808. **Vinegar.** Ocet. *AW-tsĕt.*

BREAKFAST FOODS
JÍDLA K SNÍDANI

809. **Homemade bread.** Domácí chléb.
DAW-māh-tsee khlehp.

810. **Rye bread.** Žitný chléb. *ZHĬT-nee khlēhp.*

811. White (LIT.: Wheat) bread. Pšeničný chléb.
PSHĚ-nⁱich-nee khlehp.

812. Brioche. Brioška. *BRĬ-yawsh-kah.*

813. Butter. Máslo. *MĀHS-law.*

814. Cooked cereal. Krupičná kaše.
KROO-pĭch-nah KAH-shĕ.

815. Dry cereal. Obilninové vločky.
AW-bĭl-nⁱĭ-naw-veh VLAWCH-kĭ.

816. Cracker. Suchar. *SOO-khahr.*

817. Boiled eggs. Vařená vejce.
VAH-rzhĕ-nah VAY-tsĕ.

818. Fried eggs. Smažená vejce.
SMAH-zhĕ-nah VAY-tsĕ.

819. Hard-boiled eggs. Vejce na tvrdo.
VAY-tsĕ NAH-tvŭr-daw.

820. Scrambled eggs. Míchaná vejce.
MEE-khah-nah VAY-tsĕ.

821. Soft-boiled eggs. Vejce na měkko.
VAY-tsĕ NAH-mnⁱĕ-kaw.

822. Ham and eggs. Vejce se šunkou.
VAY-tsĕ SĚ-shoon-koh‿oo.

823. Bacon and eggs. Vejce se slaninou.
VAY-tsĕ SĚ-slah-nⁱĭ-noh‿oo.

824. Jam. Džem (OR: Marmeláda).
dzhĕm (OR: *MAHR-mĕ-lah-dah*).

825. **Fruit juice.** Ovocná šťáva.
AW-vawts-nah SHT^{y}AH-vah.

826. **Grape juice.** Hroznová šťáva.
HRAWZ-naw-vah SHT^{y}AH-vah.

827. **Orange juice.** Pomerančová šťáva.
PAW-mĕ-rahn-chaw-vah SHT^{y}AH-vah.

828. **Tomato juice.** Šťáva z rajských jablíček.
SHT^{y}AH-vah ZRAH_Y-skeekh YAHB-lee-chĕk.

829. **Omelet.** Omeleta (OR: Palačinka).*
AW-mĕ-lĕ-tah (OR: *PAH-lah-chĭn-kah*).

830. **Pretzel.** Preclík. *PRĔTS-leek.*

831. **(Braided) roll.** Houska. *HOH_OOS-kah.*

832. **Flaky dough roll.** Loupáček.
LOH_OO-pah-chĕk.

833. **Kaiser roll.** Žemle. *ZHĔM-lĕh.*

834. **[Salted] crescent roll.** [Slaný] rohlík.
[SLAH-nee] RAW-hleek.

835. **Toast.** Opečený chléb (OR: Topinka).
AW-pĕ-chĕ-nee khlehp (OR: *TAW-pĭn-kah*).

Palačinky are rolled omelets made with dough, rather like crêpes.

APPETIZERS AND
HORS D'OEUVRES
PŘEDKRMY A SLANÉ
ZÁKUSKY

836. **Brains.** Mozeček. *MAW-zĕ-chĕk.*

837. **Dressed hard boiled eggs ("Eggs à la russe").** Ruská vejce. *ROO-skah VAY-tsĕ.*

838. **[Dry (**LIT.**: Hungarian)] salami.** [Uherský] salám. *[OO-her-skee] SA-lahm.*

839. **Farmer (pot) cheese.** Tvaroh. *TVAH-rawkh.*

840. **Frankfurters.** Párky.* *PAHR-kĭ.*

841. **Goose liver.** Husí játra. *HOO-see YAHT-rah.*

842. **Ham.** Šunka. *SHOON-kah.*

843. **Head cheese.** Tlačenka. *TLAH-chĕn-kah.*

844. **Knockwurst.** Buřtíky. *BOORZH-tʸee-kĭ.*

845. **Liver pâté.** Játrová paštika. *YAH-traw-vah PAHSH-tʸĭ-kah.*

846. **Open sandwiches.** Obložené chlebíčky. *AWB-law-zhĕ-neh KHLE-beech-kĭ.*

847. **Pickled mushrooms.** Houby s octem. *HOH͝OO-bĭ SAWTS-tĕm.*

848. **Radishes.** Ředkvička. *RHĔT-kvĭch-kah.*

---

* *Párky are long, thin frankfurters in pairs.*

849. **Sardines.** Sardinky. *SAHR-dĭn-kĭ.*

850. **Smoked tongue.** Uzený jazyk.
OO-zě-nee YAH-zĭk.

851. **(Sour) pickles.** Kyselé okurky.
KĬ-sě-leh AW-koor-kĭ.

852. **Sprats.** Šproty. *SHPRAW-tĭ.*

853. **Sweetbreads.** Brzlík. *BŬRZ-leek.*

854. **(Fatty) wieners.** Špekáčky. *SHPĚ-kahch-kĭ.*

SOUPS
POLÉVKY

855. **Beef broth [with liver dumplings].**
Hovězí vývar (s játrovými knedlíčky).
*HAW-vyě-zee VEE-vahr [SYAHT-raw-vee-mi
KNĚD-leech-kĭ].*

856. **Pepper pot** (LIT.: **Tripe soup**).
Dršťková polévka.
DŬRSHT ᵛ-kaw-vah PAW-lehf-kah.

857. **(Savoy) cabbage soup.** Kapustová polévka.
KAH-poos-taw-vah PAW-lehf-kah.

858. **Chicken soup.** Slepičí polévka.
SLĚ-pĭ-chee PAW-lehf-kah.

859. **Fish soup.** Rybí polévka. *RĬ-bee PAW-lehf-kah.*

860. **Lentil soup.** Čočková polévka.
CHAWCH-kaw-vah PAW-lehf-kah.

861. Mushroom soup. Houbová polévka.
HOH‿OO-baw-vah PAW-lehf-kah.

862. Pea soup. Hrachová polévka.
HRAH-khaw-vah PAW-lehf-kah.

863. Potato soup. Bramborová polévka.
BRAHM-baw-raw-vah PAW-lehf-kah.

864. Spicy meat soup. Gulášová polévka.
GOO-lah-shaw-vah PAW-lehf-kah.

865. Tomato soup. Rajská polévka.
RAH‿Y-skah PAW-lehf-kah.

866. Vegetable soup. Zeleninová polévka.
ZĔ-lĕ-nʸĭ-naw-vah PAW-lehf-kah.

SALADS
SALÁTY

867. Bean salad. Fazolový salát.
FAH-zaw-law-vee SAH-laht.

868. Beet salad. Salát z červené řepy.
SAH-laht SCHĔR-vĕ-neh RZHE-př.

869. Cucumber salad. Okurkový salát.
AW-koor-kaw-vee SAH-laht.

870. Green bean salad. Salát z fazolových lusků.
SAH-laht SFAH-zaw-law-veekh LOOS-koo.

871. **Green pepper salad.** Paprikový salát.
   PAHP-rĭ-kaw-vēē SAH-lāht.

872. **Green salad.** Hlávkový salát.
   HLĀHF-kaw-vēē SAH-lāht.

873. **Potato salad.** Bramborový salát.
   BRAHM-baw-raw-vēē SAH-lāht.

874. **Salad dressing.** Salátová marináda.
   SAH-lāh-taw-vah MAH-rĭ-nāh-dah.

875. **Tomato salad.** Salát z rajských jablíček.
   SAH-lāht ZRAH_Y skēēkh YAHB-lēē-chĕk.

GRAINS, PASTAS, DUMPLINGS
OBILNINY, TĚSTOVINY, KNEDLÍKY

876. **Buckwheat.** Kaše z pohanky.
   KAH-shĕ SPAW-hahn-kĭ.

877. **Bread dumpling.** Houskový knedlík.
   HOH_OO-skaw-vēē KNĚD-lēek.

878. **Potato dumpling.** Bramborový knedlík.
   BRAHM-baw-raw-vēē KNĚD-lēek.

879. **Macaroni.** Makarony. *MAH-kah-raw-ni.*

880. **Millet.** Prosná kaše. *PRAWS-nah KAH-shĕ.*

881. **Noodles.** Nudle. *NOOD-lĕ.*

882. **Potato pancake.** Bramborák. *BRAHM-baw-rahk.*

883. Rice. Rýže. *RĒE-zhĕ.*

884. Spaghetti. Spagety. *SPAH-gĕ-tĭ.*

MEAT AND SAUCES
MASO A OMÁČKY

885. Beef. Hovězí (maso). *HAW-vyĕ-zēe (MAH-saw).*

886. Boiled beef. Vařené hovězí (maso).
    VAH-rzhĕ-nēh HAW-vyĕ-zēe (MAH-saw).

887. Ground beef. Mleté hovězí (maso).
    MLĔ-teh HAW-vyĕ-zēe (MAH-saw).

888. Roast beef. Pečené hovězí (maso).
    PĔ-chĕ-nēh HAW-vyĕ-zēe (MAH-saw).

889. Goulash. Guláš. *GOO-lāhsh.*

890. [Thickened] gravy. [Zahuštěná] šťáva z masa.
    [ZAH-hoosh-tʸe-nāh] SHTʸĀH-vah ZMAH-sah.

891. Hare [with dark sweet sauce]. Zajíc [na černo].
    ZAH-yeets [NAH-chĕr-naw].

892. Heart. Srdce. *SŬRT-tsĕ.*

893. Lamb. Jehněčí (maso). *YĔ-hnʸĕ-chēe (MAH-saw).*

894. Liver. Játra. *YĀHT-rah.*

895. Meat. Maso. *MAH-saw.*

896. **Meatballs.** Masové knedlíčky.
  MAH-saw-veh̄ KNĚD-leech-kĭ.

897. **Meat loaf.** Sekaná pečeně.
  SĚ-kah-nah̄ PĚ-chě-nʸĕ.

898. **Mutton.** Skopové (maso).
  SKAW-paw-veh̄ (MAH-saw).

899. **Pork.** Vepřové (maso).
  VĚP-rzhaw-veh̄ (MAH-saw).

900. **Rabbit [with vegetable sauce].**
  Králík [na zelenině].
  KRAH̄-leek [NAH-zě-lě-nʸĭ-nʸĕ].

901. **Roulade.** Španělští ptáčci.
  SHPAH-nʸĕl-shtʸee PTAH̄CH-tsĭ.

902. **Roast pork, dumpling and cabbage.**
  Vepřová pečeně, knedlík a zelí.
  VĚP-rzhaw-vah̄ PĚ-chě-nʸĕ, KNĚD-leek̄ ah ZĚ-lee.

903. **Mushroom sauce.** Houbová omáčka.
  HOH‿OO-baw-vah̄ AW-mah̄ch-kah.

904. **Pickle sauce.** Okurková omáčka.
  AW-koor-kaw-vah̄ AW-mah̄ch-kah.

905. **Tomato sauce.** Rajská omáčka.
  RAH‿Y-skah̄ AW-mah̄ch-kah.

906. **Sauerbraten.** Svíčková na smetaně.
  SVEECH̄-kaw-vah NAH-smě-tah-nʸĕ.

907. **Sausage.** Klobása. *KLAW-bah̄-sah.*

908. **Blood sausage.** Jelítko. *YĚ-leet̄-kaw.*

909. **White sausage.** Jitrnice. *YĬ-tŭr-nʸĭ-tsě.*

910. **Steak.** Biftek. *BĬF-těk.*

911. **Unbreaded cutlet (Naturschnitzel).**
Přírodní řízek. *PRZHEE-rawd-nʸee RZHEE-zěk.*

912. **Veal.** Telecí (maso). *TĚ-lě-tsee (MAH-saw).*

913. **Veal cutlet.** Telecí kotleta.
TĚ-lě-tsee KAWT-lě-tah.

914. **Venison.** Srnčí (maso). *SŬRN-chee (MAH-saw).*

915. **Wiener schnitzel.** Vídeňský řízek.
VEE-děnʸ-skee RZHEE-zěk.

916. **Wild boar.** Maso z divokého kance.
MAH-saw ZDʸĬ-vaw-keh-haw KAHN-tse.

POULTRY
DRŮBEŽ

917. **Chicken.** Kuře. *KOO-rzhě.*

918. **Duck.** Kachna. *KAHKH-nah.*

919. **Goose.** Husa. *HOO-sah.*

920. **Partridge.** Koroptev. *KAW-rawp-těf.*

921. **Pheasant.** Bažant. *BAW-zhahnt.*

922. **Pigeon.** Holub. *HAW-loop.*

923. **Turkey.** Krocan. *KRAW-tsahn.*

FISH AND SEAFOOD
RYBY A MOŘSKÉ POKRMY

924. **Barbel.** Parma. *PAHR-mah.*

925. **Bass.** Mořský okoun.
MAWRZH-skee AW-koh͞oon.

926. **Carp.** Kapr. *KAH-pŭr.*

927. **Caviar.** Kaviár. *KAH-vĭ-yahr.*

928. **Clams.** Mořští mlži (OR: Zaděnky).
MAWRZH-sht ᵞee MŬL-zhĭ (OR: *ZAH-d ᵞĕn-kĭ*).

929. **Cod.** Treska. *TRĔS-kah.*

930. **Crab.** Krab. *krahp.*

931. **Eel.** Úhoř. *ŌŌ-hawrzh.*

932. **Fish fillet.** Rybí filé. *RĬ-bee FĬ-leh.*

333. **Halibut.** Platýs. *PLAH-tees.*

934. **Herring.** Sleď. *slĕt ᵞ.*

935. **Lobster.** Humr. *HOO-mŭr.*

936. **Mussels.** Mořské mušle.
MAWRZH-skeh MOOSH-lĕ.

937. **Oysters.** Ústřice. *ŌŌST-rzhĭ-tsĕ.*

938. **Perch.** Okoun. *AW-koh͞oon.*

939. **Pike.** Štika. *SHT ᵞĬ-kah.*

940. Pike perch. Candát. *TSAHN-d̄aht.*

941. Salmon. Losos. *LAW-saws.*

942. Sardine. Sardinka. *SAHR-dĭn-kah.*

943. Shrimp. Mořští ráčci (OR: Garnáti).
  MAWRZH-sht ʸee RĀHCH-tsĭ (OR: *GAHR-n̄ah-t ʸĭ*).

944. Sole. Jazír (OR: Mořský jazyk).
  YAH-z̄eer (OR: *MAWRZH-sk̄ee YAH-zĭk*).

945. Swordfish. Mečoun. *MĚ-choh‿oon.*

946. Tench. Lín. *l̄een.*

947. Trout. Pstruh. *pstrookh.*

948. Tuna. Tuňák. *TOO-nʸāhk.*

VEGETABLES
ZELENINA

949. Artichokes. Artyčoky. *AHR-tĭ-chaw-kĭ.*

950. Asparagus. Chřest. *khrzhĕst.*

951. Beans. Fazole. *FAH-zaw-lĕ.*

952. Green beans. Fazolky (OR: Fazolové lusky).
  FAH-zawl-kĭ (OR: *FAH-zaw-law-vēh LOOS-kĭ*).

953. Beets. Červená řepa. *CHĚR-vĕ-n̄ah RZHĚ-pah.*

954. Cabbage. Zelí. *ZĚ-l̄ee.*

955. **Carrots.** Mrkev. *MŬR-kĕf.*

956. **Cauliflower.** Květák. *KVYĔ-tahk.*

957. **Celery.** Celer. *TSĔ-lĕr.*

958. **Cucumbers.** Okurky. *AW-koor-kĭ.*

959. **Kohlrabi.** Kedlubny. *KĔD-loob-nĭ.*

960. **Lentil.** Čočka. *CHAWCH-kah.*

961. **Lettuce.** Hlávkový salát.
    HLĀHF-kaw-vee SAH-lāht.

962. **Mushrooms.** Houby. *HOH‿OO-bĭ.*

963. **Olives.** Olivy. *AW-lĭ-vĭ.*

964. **Onions.** Cibule. *TSĬ-boo-lĕ.*

965. **Peas.** Hrášek. *HRĀH-shĕk.*

966. **[Green] peppers.** [Zelená] paprika.
    [ZĔ-lĕ-nāh] PAHP-rĭ-kah.

967. **[Baked] potatoes.** [Pečené] brambory.
    [PĔ-chĕ-nēh] BRAHM-baw-rĭ.

968. **Boiled potatoes.** Vařené brambory.
    VAH-rzhĕ-nēh BRAHM-baw-rĭ.

969. **French fried potatoes.** Pommes frites.
    PAWM-frĭt.

970. **Fried potatoes.** Smažené brambory.
    SMAH-zhĕ-nēh BRAHM-baw-rĭ.

971. **Home fried potatoes.** Opékané brambory.
    AW-peh-kah-nēh BRAHM-baw-rĭ.

972. **Mashed potatoes.** Bramborová kaše.
 BRAHM-baw-raw-vah KAH-shĕ.

973. **Stuffed potatoes.** Nadívané brambory.
 NAH-dᵛee-vah-neh BRAHM-baw-rĭ.

974. **Spinach.** Špenát. *SHPĔ-naht.*

975. **Tomatoes.** Rajská jablíčka.
 RAH‿Y-skah YAHB-leech-kah.

FRUITS
OVOCE

976. **Apple.** Jablko. *YAH-bŭl-kaw.*

977. **Apricots.** Meruňky. *MĔ-roonᵛ-kĭ.*

978. **Banana.** Banán. *BAH-nahn.*

979. **Blueberries.** Borůvky. *BAW-roof-kĭ.*

980. **Cantaloupe.** Ananasový meloun.
 AH-nah-nah-saw-vee MĔ-loh‿oon.

981. **Cherries.** Třešně. *TRZHĔSH-nᵛĕ.*

982. **Sour cherries.** Višně. *VĬSH-nᵛĕ.*

983. **Currants.** Rybíz. *RĬ-bees.*

984. **Dates.** Datle. *DAHT-lĕ.*

985. **Figs.** Fíky. *FEE-kĭ.*

986. **Filberts** (OR: **Hazelnuts**). Lískové ořechy.
LEES-kaw-veh AW-rzhĕ-khĭ.

987. **Gooseberries.** Angrešt. *AHN-grĕsht.*

988. **A half grapefruit.** Půlka grapefruitu.
POOL-kah GRAYP-froo-too.

989. **Grapes.** Hrozny vína. *HRAWZ-nĭ VEE-nah.*

990. **Lemon.** Citrón. *TSĬT-rawn.*

991. **Mango.** Mango. *MAHN-gaw.*

992. **Orange.** Pomeranč. *PAW-mĕ-rahnch.*

993. **Peach.** Broskev. *BRAWS-kĕf.*

994. **Pears.** Hruška. *HROOSH-kah.*

995. **Peanuts.** Burské oříšky.
BOOR-skeh AW-rzheesh-kĭ.

996. **Pineapple.** Ananas. *AH-nah-nahs.*

997. **Plums.** Švestky. *SHVĔST-kĭ.*

998. **Prunes.** Sušené švestky. *SOO-shĕ-neh SHVĔST-kĭ.*

999. **Raspberries.** Maliny. *MAH-lĭ-nĭ.*

1000. **Rhubarb.** Reveň (OR: Rebarbora).
RĔ-vĕn^y (OR: RĔ-bahr-baw-rah).

1001. **Strawberries.** Jahody. *YAH-haw-dĭ.*

1002. **Wild strawberries.** Lesní jahody.
LĔS-n^yee YAH-haw-dĭ.

1003. **Tangerine.** Mandarinka. *MAHN-dah-rĭn-kah.*

1004. **Walnuts.** Vlašské ořechy.
   VLAHSH-skeh AW-rzhĕ-khĭ.

1005. **Watermelon.** Meloun. *MĔ-loh‿oon.*

DESSERTS AND CHEESES
MOUČNÍKY A SÝRY

1006. **Apple strudel.** Jablkový závin.
   YAH-bŭl-kaw-vee ZAH-vĭn.

1007. **Cake.** Buchta. *BOOKH-tah.*

1008. **Rich cake (torte).** Dort. *dawrt.*

1009. **Beer cheese.** Syrečky (OR: Tvarůžky).
   SĬ-rĕch-kĭ (OR: TVAH-roosh-kĭ).

1010. **Blue cheese.** Plísňový sýr. *PLEES-nʸaw-vee seer.*

1011. **Cream cheese.** Krémový sýr (OR: Žervé).
   KREH-maw-vee seer (OR: ZHĔR-veh).

1012. **Limburger cheese.** Limburský sýr.
   LĬM-boor-skee seer.

1013. **Mild cheese.** Jemný sýr. *YĔM-nee seer.*

1014. **Sheep cheese.** Brynza. *BRĬN-zah.*

1015. **Strong cheese.** Ostrý sýr. *AWST-ree seer.*

1016. **Swiss cheese.** Ementálský sýr.
   Ĕ-mĕn-tahl-skee seer.

1017. Cookies. Cukroví (OR: Sušenky).
TSOO-kraw-vee (OR: *SOO-shĕn-kĭ*).

1018. Custard. Krém. *krehm.*

1019. Doughnuts. Koblihy. *KAWB-lĭ-hĭ.*

1020. French pastry. Dortové řezy.
DAWR-taw-veh RZHĔ-zĭ.

1021. Fruit dumplings. Ovocné knedlíky.
AW-vawts-neh KNĔD-lee-kĭ.

1022. Ice cream. Zmrzlina. *ZMŬR-zlĭ-nah.*

1023. Chocolate ice cream. Čokoládová zmrzlina.
CHAW-kaw-lah-daw-vah ZMŬR-zlĭ-nah.

1024. Mocca ice cream (LIT: Frozen coffee).
Mražená káva. *MRAH-zhĕ-nah KAH-vah.*

1025. Vanilla ice cream. Vanilková zmrzlina.
VAH-nĭl-kaw-vah ZMŬR-zlĭ-nah.

1026. Gingerbread. Perník. *PĔR-nʸeek.*

1027. Kugelhupf. Bábovka. *BAH-bawf-kah.*

1028. Pancakes. Palačinky (OR: Lívance).*
PAH-lah-chĭn-kĭ (OR: *LEE-vahn-tsĕ*).

1029. Pie. Koláč. *KAW-lahch.*

1030. Pudding. Pudink. *POO-dink.*

1031. Roquefort. Rokfór. *RAWK-fawr.*

1032. Soufflé. Nákyp. *NAH-kĭp.*

* *Lívance* are flat, *palačinky* are rolled.

1033. **Sweet buns** (**"Little pies"**). Koláčky.
KAW-lahch-kǐ.

1034. **Whipped cream.** Šlehačka. *SHLĚ-hahch-kah.*

1035. **Zabaglione.** Šodó. *SHAW-daw.*

BEVERAGES
NÁPOJE

1036. **[Hot] chocolate.** [Horké] kakao.
[HAWR-keh] KAH-kah-aw.

1037. **Coffee.** Káva. *KAH-vah.*

1038. **Black coffee.** Černá káva. *CHĚR-nah KAH-vah.*

1039. **With sugar.** S cukrem. *STSOOK-rĕm.*

1040. **Without sugar.** Bez cukru. *BĚS-tsook-roo.*

1041. **With cream.** Se smetanou. *SĚ-smĕ-tah-noh‿oo.*

1042. **Milk.** Mléko. *MLEH-kaw.*

1043. **[Hot] tea.** [Horký] čaj. *[HAWR-kee] chah‿y.*

1044. **Iced tea.** Čaj s ledem. *chah‿y SLĚ-dĕm.*

1045. **Tea with milk.** Čaj s mlékem.
chah‿y SMLEH-kem.

1046. **Water [with ice].** Voda [s ledem].
VAW-dah [SLĚ-dĕm].

1047. **— without ice.** — bez ledu. — *BĚZ-lĕ-doo.*

See also "Café and Bar," p. 97.

SIGHTSEEING
PROHLÍDKA PAMÁTEK

1048. **I want a licensed guide who speaks English.**

Chci uznaného průvodce, který mluví anglicky.

khtsĭ OO-znah-nĕh-haw PROO-vawt-tsĕ, KTĔ-ree MLOO-vee AHN-glĭts-kĭ.

1049. **How long will the entire excursion take?**

Jak dlouho bude trvat celá prohlídka?

yahk DLOH‿OO-haw BOO-dĕ TŬR-vaht TSĔ-lah PRAW-hlĕet-kah?

1050. **Are admission tickets and lunch included?**

Je v tom započteno vstupné a polední jídlo?

yĕ ftawm ZAH-pawch-tĕ-naw FSTOOP-neh ah PAW-lĕd-nʸee YEED-law?

1051. **What is the charge for a trip [to the Konopiště castle]?**

Kolik stojí zájezd [na zámek Konopiště]?

KAW-lĭk STAW-yee ZAH-yĕst [NA-zah-mĕk KAW-naw-pĭsh-tʸĕ]?

1052. **— to the Beskydy Mountains.**

— do Beskyd. — *DAW-bĕs-kĭt.*

1053. — to Mácha's Lake.
    — k Máchovu jezeru.
    — *KMĀH-khaw-voo YĔ-zĕ-roo.*

1054. **What is the charge for a trip [around the city]?**
    Kolik stojí projížďka [městem]?
    KAW-lĭk   STAW-yēe   PRAW-yeeshtʸ-kah [MNʸĔS-tĕm]?

1055. — to the suburbs (OR: environs)?
    — po okolí? — *PAW-aw-kaw-lēe?*

1056. **Call for me tomorrow at my hotel at 8 A.M.**
    Zastavte se pro mne před mým hotelem v osm hodin ráno.
    ZAH-stahf-tĕ-sĕ PRAW-mně PRZĔD-mēem HAW-tĕ-lĕm VAW-soom HAW-dʸĭn RĀH-naw.

1057. **Show me the sights of interest.**
    Ukažte mi místní pozoruhodnosti.
    OO-kahsh-tĕ mĭ MĒEST-nʸee PAW-zaw-roo-hawd-naws-tʸĭ.

1058. **What is [this building]?**
    Co je [tato budova]?
    tsaw yĕ [TAH-taw BOO-daw-vah]?

1059. **How old is it?**
    Jak je to staré?
    yahk yĕ taw STAH-reh?

1060. **I am interested [in architecture].**
Zajímám se [o stavitelství].
ZAH-yee-mahm-sĕ [AW-stah-vĭ-tĕls-tvee].

1061. **— in archeology.** — o archeologii.
— AW-ahr-khĕ-aw-law-gĭ-yĭ.

1062. **— in sculpture.** — o sochařství.
— AW-saw-khahrzhs-tvee.

1063. **— in painting.** — o malířství.
— AW-mah-leerzhs-tvee.

1064. **— in graphic arts.** — o grafiku.
— AW-grah-fĭ-koo.

1065. **— in native arts and crafts.**
— o lidové umění a domácká řemesla.
— AW-lĭ-daw-veh OO-mnᵘĕ-nᵘee ah DAW-mahts-kah RZHĔ-mĕs-lah.

1066. **— in contemporary painting.**
— o současné malířství.
— AW-soh‿oo-chahs-neh MAH-leerzhs-tvee.

1067. **— in modern art.** — o moderní umění.
— AW-maw-dĕr-nᵘee OO-mnᵘĕ-nᵘee.

1068. **I would like to see [the park].**
Rád bych viděl [park].
RAHD-bĭkh VĬ-dᵘĕl [pahrk].

1069. **— the cathedral.**
— katedrálu (or: chrám).
— KAH-tĕd-rah-loo (or: khrahm).

1070. — **the library.** — knihovnu.
— *KN^yǏ-hawv-noo.*

1071. — **the ruins.** — zříceniny.
— *ZRZHEE-tsĕ-n^yĭ-nĭ.*

1072. — **the castle.** — zámek (OR: hrad).
— *ZAH-mĕk* (OR: *hraht*).

1073. — **the palace.** — palác. — *PAH-lahts.*

1074. — **the zoo.**
— zoologickou zahradu (OR: zoo).
— *ZAW-aw-law-gĭts-koh͜oo ZAH-hrah-doo* (OR: *ZAW-aw*).

1075. Let's take a walk [around the botanical garden].
Projděme se [po botanické zahradě].
PROY-d^yĕ-mĕ-sĕ [PAW-baw-tah-nĭts-keh ZAH-hrah-d^yĕ].

1076. A beautiful view!
To je překrásný pohled!
taw yĕ PRZHĔ-krahs-nee PAW-hlĕt!

1077. Very interesting!
To je velmi zajímavé!
taw yĕ VĔL-mĭ ZAH-yee-mah-veh!

1078. Magnificent!
To je nádherné!
taw yĕ NAHD-hĕr-neh!

1079. **I am enjoying myself.**
Bavím se velmi dobře.
BAH-veem-sĕ VĔL-mĭ DAWB-rzhĕ.

1080. **I am bored.**
Nudím se.
NOO-dʸeem-sĕ.

1081. **When does the museum [open] close?**
Kdy se [otvírá] zavírá muzeum?
GDĬ-sĕ [AWT-vee-rah] ZAH-vee-rah MOO-zĕ-oom?

1082. **Is this the way [to the entrance]?**
Dostanu se tudy [ke vchodu]?
DAW-stah-noo-sĕ TOO-dĭ [KĔ-fkhaw-doo]?

1083. **— to the exit.** — k východu.
— KVEE-khaw-doo.

1084. **Let's visit the fine arts gallery.**
Pojďme navštívit galerii výtvarných umění.
POYDʸ-mĕ NAHF-shtʸee-vĭt GAH-lĕ-rĭ-yĭ VEE-tvahr-neekh OO-mnʸĕ-nʸee.

1085. **Let's stay longer.**
Zůstaňme ještě.
ZOO-stahnʸ-mĕ YĔSH-tʸĕ.

1086. **Let's leave now.**
Pojďme už.
POYDʸ-mĕ oosh.

1087. **If there is time, let's rest a while.**
Jestli máme čas, odpočiňme si chvíli.
*YĔST-lĭ MĀH-mĕ chahs, AWT-paw-chĭnᵘ-
mĕ-sĭ KHVĒE-lĭ.*

WORSHIP
BOHOSLUŽBY

1088. **Altar.** Oltář. *AWL-tahʳzh.*

1089. **Cathedral.** Katedrála (OR: Chrám).
KAH-tĕd-rah̄-lah (OR: *khrah̄m*).

1090. **Catholic church.** Katolický kostel.
KAH-taw-lĭts-kēe KAWS-tĕl.

1091. **Choral music.** Sborová hudba.
ZBAW-raw-vah̄ HOOD-bah.

1092. **Confession.** Zpověď. *SPAW-vyĕtᵘ.*

1093. **Contribution.** Příspěvek. *PRZHĒE-spyĕ-vĕk.*

1090. **Mass.** Mše. *mshĕ.*

1095. **Minister.** Duchovní. *DOO-khawv-nᵘēe.*

1096. **Prayers.** Modlitby. *MAWD-lĭd-bĭ.*

1097. **Prayer book.** Modlitební knížka.
MAWD-lĭ-tĕb-nᵘēe KNᵘĒESH-kah.

1098. **Priest.** Kněz. *knᵘĕs.*

1099. **Protestant church.** Protestantský kostel.
    PRAW-těs-tahnt-skee KAWS-těl.

1100. **Rabbi.** Rabín. *RAH-been.*

1101. **Synagogue.** Synagoga. *SI-nah-gaw-gah.*

1102. **Sermon.** Kázání. *KAH-zah-n^yee.*

1103. **Services.** Obřady (or: Bohoslužby).
    AWB-rzhah-dǐ (or: *BAW-haw-sloozh-bǐ*).

ENTERTAINMENTS
ZÁBAVA

1104. **Is there a [matinee] today?**
    Je dnes [odpolední představení]?
    *yě dněs [AWT-paw-lěd-n^yee PRZHĚT-stah-
    vě-n^yee]?*

1105. **Has [the show] begun?**
    Začalo už [představení]?
    ZAH-chah-law oosh [PRZHĚT-stah-vě-n^yee]?

1106. **What is playing now?**
    Co se teď dává?
    TSAW-sě tět^y DAH-vah?

1107. **Have you any seats for tonight?**
    Máte nějaké lístky na dnes večer?
    *MAH-tě N^yĚ-yah-keh LEEST-kǐ NAH-dněs
    VĚ-chěr?*

1108. How much is [an orchestra seat]?
Kolik stojí [lístek do přízemí]?
KAW-lik STAW-yee [LEES-těk DAW-przhee-
zě-mee]?

1109. — a balcony seat. — lístek na balkón.
— LEES-těk NAH-bahl-kawn.

1110. — a box. — lístek do lóže.
— LEES-těk DAW-law-zhě.

1111. Not too far from the stage.
Ne příliš daleko od jeviště.
ně PRZHEE-lǐsh DAH-lě-kaw AWD-yě-vǐsh-
tʸě.

1112. Can I see and hear well from there?
Budu odtamtud dobře vidět a slyšet?
BOO-doo AWT-tahm-toot DAWB-rzhě VǏ-
dʸět ah SLǏ-shět?

1113. When does the program start?
Kdy začíná program?
gdǐ ZAH-chee-nah PRAW-grahm?

1114. When does the program end?
Kdy končí program?
gdǐ KAWN-chee PRAW-grahm?

1115. How long is the intermission?
Jak dlouho trvá přestávka?
yahk DLOH_OO-haw TŮR-vah PRZHĚ-
stahf-kah?

1116. **The ballet.**
Balet.
BAH-lĕt.

1117. **The box office.**
Pokladna.
PAW-klahd-nah.

1118. **The circus.**
Cirkus.
TSĬR-koos.

1119. **A concert.**
Koncert.
KAWN-tsĕrt.

1120. **The folk dances.**
Lidové tance.
LĬ-daw-veh TAHN-tsĕ.

1121. **The gambling casino.**
Herna.
HĔR-nah.

1122. **The line** (OR: **queue**).
Fronta.
FRAWN-tah.

1123. **The movies.**
Kino (OR: Biograf).
KĬ-naw (OR: *BĬ-yaw-grahf*).

1124. **The musical comedy.**
Muzikál.
MOO-zi-kahl.

1125. The nightclub.
Noční podnik.
NAWCH-nʸee PAWD-nʸĭk.

1126. The opera.
Opera.
AW-pĕ-rah.

1127. Opera glasses.
Divadelní kukátko.
DʸĬ-vah-dĕl-nʸee KOO-kaht-kaw.

1128. The performance.
Představení.
PRZHĔT-stah-vĕ-nʸee.

1129. The program.
Program.
PRAW-grahm.

1130. A puppet show.
Loutkové divadlo.
LOH‿OOT-kaw-veh DʸĬ-vahd-law.

1131. Reserved seat.
Číslované místo.
CHEES-law-vah-neh MEES-taw.

1132. Sports arena.
Sportovní hala.
SPAWR-tawv-nʸee HAH-lah.

1133. Sports event.
Sportovní podnik.
SPAWR-tawv-nʸee PAWD-nʸĭk.

1134. Standing room.
Místo k stání.
MĒES-taw KSTĀH-nʸēe.

1135. The theater.
Divadlo.
DʸĬ-vahd-law.

1136. The ticket window.
Přepážka pokladny (OR: Předprodej lístků).
PRZHĔ-pāhsh-kah   PAW-klahd-nǐ   (OR:
PRZHĔT-praw-day LĒEST-koo).

1137. This ticket.
Tento lístek.
TĔN-taw LĒES-tĕk.

1138. The usher.
Uváděč (FEMININE: Uváděčka).
OO-vah-dʸĕch (FEMININE: OO-vah-dʸĕch-kah).

1139. The variety show.
Varieté.
VAH-rĭ-yĕ-tēh.

NIGHTCLUB AND DANCING
NOČNÍ PODNIKY A TANEC

1140. What is the admission charge?
Kolik se platí vstupné?
KAW-lĭk-sĕ PLAH-tʸēe FSTOOP-neh?

1141. What is the cover charge?
Jak velká je tu režijní přirážka?
yahk VĔL-kah yĕ too RĔ-zhee‿y-nʸee PRZHĬ-rahsh-kah?

1142. What is the minimum charge?
Jak velká musí být minimální útrata?
yahk VĔL-kah MOO-see beet MĬ-nĭ-mahl-nʸee OO-trah-tah?

1143. Is there a floor show?
Je zde nějaký program?
yĕ zdĕ NʸĔ-yah-kee PRAW-grahm?

1144. Where can we go to dance?
Kam si můžeme jít zatančit?
KAHM-sĭ MOO-zhĕ-mĕ yeet ZAH-tahn-chĭt?

1145. May I have this dance (LIT.: **May I ask**)**?**
Smím prosit?
smeem PRAW-sĭt?

1146. You dance very well.
Tančíte velmi dobře.
TAHN-chee-tĕ VĔL-mĭ DAWB-rzhĕ.

1147. Will you play [a fox trot]?
Budete hrát [foxtrot]?
BOO-de-te hraht [FAWKS-trawt]?

1148. — a rumba. — rumbu. — *ROOM-boo.*

1149. — a samba. — sambu. — *SAHM-boo.*

1150. — a tango. — tango. — *TAHN-gaw.*

1151. — **a waltz.** — valčík. — *VAHL-cheek.*

1152. — **a folk dance.** — lidový tanec.
— *LĬ-daw-vee TAH-něts.*

1153. — **rock music.** — rokenrol.
— *RAWK-ěn-rawl.*

SPORTS
SPORTY

1154. **We want to play [soccer].**
Chtěli bychom si zahrát [kopanou].
KHT^yĔ-li BĬ-khawm-si ZAH-hraht [KAW-pah-noh‿oo].

1155. — **basketball.** — košíkovou.
— *KAW-shee-kaw-voh‿oo.*

1156. — **golf.** — golf. — *gawlf.*

1157. — **ping pong.**
— stolní tenis (OR: ping pong).
— *STAWL-n^yee TĚ-nĭs (OR: pĭng pawng).*

1158. — **tennis.** — tenis. — *TĚ-nĭs.*

1159. — **volleyball.**
— volejbal (OR: odbíjenou).
— *VAW-lay-bahl (OR: AWD-bee-yě-noh‿oo).*

1160. Let's go swimming.
Pojďme si zaplavat.
POYD<sup>y</sup>-mě-sĭ ZAH-plah-vaht.

1161. Let's go [to the swimming pool].
Pojďme [na koupaliště].
POYD<sup>y</sup>-mě [NAH-koh‿oo-pah-lĭsh-t<sup>y</sup>ě].

1162. — to the beach. — na pláž.
— NAH-plāhsh.

1163. — to the horse races.
— na koňské dostihy.
— NAH-kawn<sup>y</sup>-skeh DAW-st<sup>y</sup>ĭ-hĭ.

1164. — to the soccer game.
— na fotbalový zápas.
— NAH-fawd-bah-law-vee ZĀH-pahs.

1165. I need [equipment].
Potřebuji [výstroj].
PAW-trzhě-boo-yĭ [VĒĒ-stroy].

1166. — fishing tackle. — rybářské náčiní.
— RĬ-bāhrzh-skeh NĀH-chĭ-n<sup>y</sup>ee.

1167. — a tennis racket. — tenisovou raketu.
— TĚ-nĭ-saw-voh‿oo RAH-kě-too.

1168. Can we go [fishing]?
Můžeme jít [na ryby]?
MŌŌ-zhě-mě yeet [NAH-rĭ-bĭ]?

1169. — **horseback riding.**
   — na projížďku na koni.
   — *NAH-praw-yeesht^y-koo NAH-kaw-n^yĭ.*

1170. — **roller skating.**
   — bruslit na kolečkových bruslích.
   — *BROOS-lĭt   NAH-kaw-lěch-kaw-veekh BROOS-leekh.*

1171. — **ice skating.** — bruslit. — *BROOS-lĭt.*

1172. — **skiing.** — lyžovat. — *LĬ-zhaw-vaht.*

BANK AND MONEY
BANKA A PENÍZE

1173. **Where can I change foreign money?**
   Kde dostanu vyměnit cizí valutu?
   gdě DAW-stah-noo VĬ-mn^yě-n^yĭt TSĬ-zee VAH-loo-too?

1174. **What is the exchange rate on the dollar?**
   V jakém poměru se vyměňuje dolar?
   VYAH-kehm PAW-mn^yě-roo-sě VĬ-mn^yě-n^yoo- yě DAW-lahr?

1175. Will you cash [a personal check]?
Rozměnil byste mi [osobní šek]?
RAWZ-mnyě-nyǐl BĬS-tě mǐ [AW-sawb-nyee shěk]?

1176. — a traveler's check. — cestovní šek.
— TSĚS-tawv-nyee shěk.

1177. I have [a bank draft].
Mám [bankovní směnku].
mahm [BAHN-kawv-nyee SMNyĚN-koo].

1178. — a letter of credit. — akreditiv.
— AH-krě-dǐ-teef.

1179. — traveler's checks. — cestovní šeky.
— TSĚS-tawv-nyee SHĚ-kǐ.

1180. I would like to exchange twenty dollars for Czechoslovak currency.
Rád bych vyměnil dvacet dolarů za československé peníze.
RAHD-bǐkh VĬ-mnyě-nyǐl DVAH-tsět DAW-lah-roo ZAH-chěs-kaw-slaw-věn-skeh PĚ-nyee-zě.

1181. Please change this [for large bills (LIT: for bills of higher value)].
Vyměňte mi toto laskavě [za bankovky vyšší hodnoty].
VĬ-mnyěny-tě mǐ TAW-taw LAHS-kah-vyě [ZAH-bahn-kawf-kǐ VĬSH-shee HAWD-naw-tǐ].

1182. — **for small bills** (LIT.: **for bills of lower value**).
— za bankovky nižší hodnoty.
— *ZAH-bahn-kawf-kǐ Nʸ ĬSH-sheē HAWD-naw-tǐ.*

1183. — **for small change.** — za drobné.
— *ZAH-drawb-neh.*

SHOPPING
NAKUPOVÁNÍ

1184. **I need [a sports shirt].**
Potřebuji [sportovní košili].
PAW-trzhě-boo-yǐ [SPAWR-tawv-nʸeē KAW-shǐ-lǐ].

1185. **I have been waiting [a long time].**
Čekám (zde) [už dlouho].
CHĚ-kāhm (zdě) [oosh DLOH‿OO-haw].

1186. — **a short time.** — krátkou dobu.
— *KRĀHT-koh‿oo DAW-boo.*

1187. **Show me [the hat] in the window.**
Ukažte mi [ten klobouk] ve výkladní skříni.
OO-kahsh-tě mǐ [ten KLAW-boh‿ook] VĚ-vee-klahd-nʸeē SKRZHEē-nʸǐ.

1188. **I am just looking around** (LIT.: **I am only looking at what you have here**).
Pouze si prohlížím, co tu máte.
POH‿OO-zě-sǐ PRAW-hlee-zheem, tsaw too MAH-tě.

1189. **I'll wait until it is ready.**
Počkám, až to bude připraveno.
PAWCH-kǎhm, ahsh taw BOO-dě PRZHĬprah-vě-naw.

1190. **I shall come back later.**
Stavím se později.
STAH-veem-sě PAWZ-dʸě-yǐ.

1191. **What brand do you have?**
Jakou značku máte?
YAH-koh‿oo ZNAHCH-koo MAH-tě?

1192. **How much is it?**
Kolik to stojí?
KAW-lǐk taw STAW-yee?

1193. **How much is it [per piece]?**
Kolik stojí [kus]?
KAW-lǐk STAW-yee [koos]?

1194. **— per meter.** — metr. — *MĚ-tǔr.*

1195. **— per pound.** — libra. — *LĬB-rah.*

1196. **— per kilo.** — kilo. — *KĬ-law.*

1197. **— per package.** — balíček.
— *BAH-lee-chěk.*

1198. — **per bunch.** — svazek. — *SVAH-zĕk.*

1199. **How much is it all together?**
Kolik to stojí všechno dohromady?
*KAW-lĭk taw STAW-yeē FSHĔKH-naw
DAW-hraw-mah-dĭ?*

1200. **It is [too expensive].**
Je to [příliš drahé].
yĕ taw [PRZHĒE-lĭsh DRAH-hĕh].

1201. — **cheap.** — laciné. — *LAH-tsĭ-nĕh.*

1202. — **reasonable.** — za přijatelnou cenu.
— *ZAH-przhĭ-yah-tĕl-noh_oo TSĔ-noo.*

1203. **Is that your lowest price?**
Je to vaše nejnižší cena?
yĕ taw VAH-shĕ NAY-nᵘĭsh-sheē TSĔ-nah?

1204. **Can I get a discount?**
Mohu dostat slevu?
MAW-hoo DAW-staht SLĔ-voo?

1205. **I like that.**
Líbí se mi to.
LĒE-bee-sĕ mĭ taw.

1206. **I do not like that.**
Nelíbí se mi to.
NĔ-lee-bee-sĕ mĭ taw.

1207. **Have you something [better]?**
Máte něco [lepšího]?
MĀH-tĕ NᵘĔ-tsaw [LĔP-shee-haw]?

1208. — **cheaper.** — levnějšího.
— *LĚV-nʸay-shee-haw.*

1209. — **more chic.** — elegantnějšího.
— *Ě-lě-gahnt-nʸay-shee-haw.*

1210. — **softer.** — měkčího. — *MNʸĚK-chee-haw.*

1211. — **stronger.** — pevnějšího.
— *PĚV-nʸay-shee-haw.*

1212. — **lighter** (**in weight**). — lehčího.
— *LĚKH-chee-haw.*

1213. — **tighter.** — těsnějšího.
— *TʸĚS-nʸay-shee-haw.*

1214. — **looser.** — volnějšího.
— *VAWL-nʸay-shee-haw.*

1215. — **lighter** (**in color**). — světlejšího.
— *SVYĚT-lay-shee-haw.*

1216. — **darker.** — tmavšího.
— *TMAHF-shee-haw.*

1217. **Show me something [in a medium size].**
Ukažte mi něco [ve středním čísle].
OO-kahsh-tě mĭ NʸĚ-tsaw [VĚ-strzhěd-nʸeem CHEES-lě].

1218. — **in a large size.** — ve velkém čísle.
— *VĚ-věl-kehm CHEES-lě.*

1219. — **in a small size.** — v malém čísle.
— *VMAH-lehm CHEES-lě.*

1220. — **in another color.** — v jiné barvě.
— *VYĬ-neh BAHR-vyě.*

1221. — **in a different style.** — v jiném střihu.
— *VYĬ-nehm STRZHĬ-hoo.*

1222. **May I try it on?**
Mohu si to zkusit?
MAW-hoo-sĭ taw SKOO-sĭt?

1223. **Can I order the same thing [in my size]?**
Mohu si objednat totéž [v mém čísle]?
MAW-hoo-sĭ AWB-yěd-naht TAW-těhsh [vmehm CHEES-lě]?

1224. **Take the measurements.**
Změřte mne.
ZMNʸĚRZH-tě mně.

1225. **Measure [the length].**
Změřte [délku].
ZMNʸĚRZH-tě [DEHL-koo].

1226. — **the width.** — šířku. — *SHEERZH-koo.*

1227. **Will it shrink?**
Sráží se to?
SRAH-zhee-sě taw?

1228. Will it break?
Láme se to?
LAH̄-mĕ-sĕ taw?

1229. Will it rip?
Trhá se to?
TŬR-hah-sĕ taw?

1230. Is it [new]?
Je to [nové]?
yĕ taw [NAW-vēh]?

1231. — second hand. — příležitostná koupě.
    — PRZHĒE-lĕ-zhĭ-tawst-nah KOH‿OO-
       pyĕ.

1232. — an antique. — starožitnost.
    — STAH-raw-zhĭt-nawst.

1233. — a replica. — kopie. — *KAW-pĭ-yĕ.*

1234. — an imitation. — imitace.
    — Ĭ-mĭ-tah-tsĕ.

1235. Is this color-fast?
Nepouští to?
NĔ-poh‿oosh-tʸēe taw?

1236. This is my size.
Toto je moje velikost.
TAW-taw yĕ MAW-yĕ VĔ-lĭ-kawst.

1237. This is not my size.
Toto není moje velikost.
TAW-taw NĔ-nʸēe MAW-yĕ VĔ-lĭ-kawst.

1238. Please have this ready soon.
Připravte mi to, prosím, brzy.
PRZHĬ-prahf-tě mĭ taw, PRAW-seem, BŬR-zĭ.

1239. How long will it take to make the alterations?
Za jak dlouho mi to budete moci přešít?
ZAH-yahk DLOH͜OO-haw mĭ taw BOO-dě-tě MAW-tsĭ PRZHĚ-sheet?

1240. Wrap this.
Zabalte mi to.
ZAH-bahl-tě mĭ taw.

1241. Where do I pay?
Kde budu platit?
gdě BOO-doo PLAH-tʸĭt?

1242. Do I pay [the salesman]?
Budu platit [prodavači]?
BOO-doo PLAH-tʸĭt [PRAW-dah-vah-chĭ]?

1243. — the salesgirl. — prodavačce.
— *PRAW-dah-vahch-tsě.*

1244. — the cashier.
— pokladní (MALE: pokladnímu).
—- *PAW-klahd-nʸee (PAW-klahd-nʸee-moo).*

1245. Will you honor this credit card?
Přijímáte tento úvěrový průkaz?
PRZHĬ-yee-mah-tě TĚN-taw OO-vyě-raw-vee PROO-kahs?

1246. May I pay with a personal check?
Mohu platit osobním šekem?
MAW-hoo PLAH-t^yit AW-sawb-n^yeem SHĚ-kĕm?

1247. Is this identification acceptable?
Stačí tento průkaz totožnosti?
STAH-chee̅ TĚN-taw PROO̅-kahs TAW-tawzh-naws-t^yĭ?

1248. Is the reference sufficient?
Postačují tyto reference?
PAW-stah-choo-yee̅ TĬ-taw RĚ-fĕ-rĕn-tsĕ?

1249. Can you send it to my hotel?
Můžete mi to poslat do hotelu?
MOO̅-zhĕ-tĕ mĭ taw PAW-slaht DAW-haw-tĕ-loo?

1250. Can you ship it [to New York City]?
Můžete (mi) to odeslat [do New Yorku]?
MOO̅-zhĕ-tĕ (mĭ) taw AW-dĕ-slaht [DAW-n^yoo-yawr-koo]?

1251. Pack this carefully for export.
Zabalte to pečlivě k vývozu.
ZAH-bahl-tĕ taw PĚCH-lĭ-vyĕ KVEE̅-vaw-zoo.

1252. Give me [a bill].
Dejte mi [účet].
DAY-tĕ mĭ [OO̅-chĕt].

1253. — **a receipt.** — stvrzenku.
— *STVŬR-zĕn-koo.*

1254. Send it to me C.O.D.
Pošlete mi to na dobírku.
PAW-shlĕ-tĕ mĭ taw NAH-daw-beer-koo.

1255. Is there an additional charge [for delivery]?
Účtujete zvlášť [za doručení]?
$\overline{OO}$*CH-too-yĕ-tĕ zvl*$\overline{a}$*hsht*^{y} [*ZAH-daw-roo-chĕ-n*^{y}*ee*]*?*

CLOTHING AND ACCESSORIES
ŠATY A DOPLŇKY

1256. A bathing cap. Koupací čapka.
KOH_OO-pah-ts$\overline{ee}$ *CHAHP-kah.*

1257. A bathing suit. Plavky. *PLAHF-kĭ.*

1258. A blouse. Blůza (OR: Halenka).
BL$\overline{OO}$*-zah* (OR: *HAH-lĕn-kah*).

1259. A belt. Opasek. *AW-pah-sĕk.*

1260. Boots. Boty. *BAW-tĭ.*

1261. A bracelet. Náramek. *N*$\overline{AH}$*-rah-mĕk.*

1262. A brassiere. Podprsenka. *PAWT-pŭr-sĕn-kah.*

1263. A cane. Hůl. $\overline{hool}$.

1264. A coat. Kabát. *KAH-b*$\overline{aht}$.

1265. A collar. Límec. *L*$\overline{EE}$*-mĕts.*

1266. Cufflinks. Manžetové knoflíčky.
MAHN-zhĕ-taw-veh KNAW-fleech-kĭ.

1267. Diapers. Dětské plenky.
DᵛĔTS-keh PLĔN-kĭ.

1268. A dress. Šaty. *SHAH-tĭ.*

1269. Children's dresses. Dětské šaty.
DᵞĔTS-keh SHAH-tĭ.

1270. Earrings. Náušnice. *NĀH-oosh-nᵞĭ-tse.*

1271. A pair of gloves. Rukavice. *ROO-kah-vĭ-tsĕ.*

1272. A handbag. Kabelka. *KAH-bĕl-kah.*

1273. A handkerchief. Kapesník. *KAH-pĕs-nᵞeek.*

1274. A hat. Klobouk. *KLAW-boh‿ook.*

1275. A jacket. Sako (OR: Žaket; OR: Kabát).
SAH-kaw (OR: ZHAH-kĕt; OR: KAH-baht).

1276. A dinner jacket. Smoking. *SMAW-kĭnk.*

1277. Jewelry. Klenoty. *KLĔ-naw-tĭ.*

1278. Lingerie. Dámské prádlo.
DĀHM-skeh PRĀHD-law.

1279. A necktie. Vázanka (OR: Kravata).
VĀH-zahn-kah (OR: KRAH-vah-tah).

1280. A necklace. Náhrdelník. *NĀH-hŭr-dĕl-nᵞeek.*

1281. A nightgown. Noční košile.
NAWCH-nᵞee KAW-shĭ-lĕ.

1282. Pajamas. Pyžama. *PĬ-zhah-mah.*

1283. Panties. Dámské kalhotky.
$\overline{DAHM}$-skeh KAHL-hawt-kǐ.

1284. A pin (decorative). Brož. *brawsh.*

1285. A raincoat. Plášť do deště.
pla͞hsht ᵘ DAW-děsh-t ᵘě.

1286. A ring. Prsten. *PŬRS-těn.*

1287. Rubbers. Galoše. *GAH-law-shě.*

1288. Sandals. Sandály. *SAHN-dah-lǐ.*

1289. A lady's scarf. Šátek. *SH$\overline{AH}$-těk.*

1290. A man's scarf. Šála. *SH$\overline{AH}$-lah.*

1291. A shirt. Košile. *KAW-shǐ-lě.*

1292. Shoes. Střevíce (OR: Polobotky).
STRZH$\overline{Ě}$-ve͞e-tsě (OR: *PAW-law-bawt-kǐ*).

1293. Shoelaces. Tkaničky do bot.
TKAH-nᵘǐch-kǐ DAW-bawt.

1294. Socks. Ponožky. *PAW-nawsh-kǐ.*

1295. Sport shorts. Šortky. *SHAWRT-kǐ.*

1296. A skirt. Sukně. *SOOK-nᵘě.*

1297. A slip. Kombiné (OR: Spodnička).
KAWM-bi-neh (OR: *SPAWD-nᵘǐch-kah*).

1298. Stockings. Punčochy. *POON-chaw-khǐ.*

1299. Man's suit. Pánský oblek.
P$\overline{AH}$N-ske͞e AWB-lěk.

1300. Lady's suit. Kostým. *KAWS-te͞em.*

1301. **A sweater.** Svetr. *SVĚ-tŭr.*

1302. **A pair of trousers.** Kalhoty. *KAHL-haw-tĭ.*

1303. **Men's underwear.** Pánské prádlo.
   PĀHN-skeh PRĀHD-law.

1304. **An umbrella.** Deštník. *DĚSHT-nᵛeek.*

1305. **An undershirt.** Tričko. *TRĬCH-kaw.*

1306. **Undershorts.** Krátké spodky.
   KRĀHT-keh SPAWT-kĭ.

COLORS
BARVY

1307. **Black.** Černý. *CHĚR-nee.*

1308. **Blue.** Modrý. *MAWD-ree.*

1309. **Brown.** Hnědý. *HNᵛĚ-dee.*

1310. **Cream.** Krémový. *KRĒH-maw-vee.*

1311. **Grey.** Šedý. *SHĚ-dee.*

1312. **Green.** Zelený. *ZĚ-lĕ-nee.*

1313. **Olive.** Olivový. *AW-lĭ-vaw-vee.*

1314. **Orange.** Oranžový. *AW-rahn-zhaw-vee.*

1315. **Pink.** Růžový. *RŌO-zhaw-vee.*

1316. **Purple.** Fialový. *FĬ-yah-law-vee.*

1317. Red. Červený. *CHĚR-vĕ-nee.*

1318. Tan. Žlutohnědý. *ZHLOO-taw-hn^yĕ-dee.*

1319. White. Bílý. *BEE-lee.*

1320. Yellow. Žlutý. *ZHLOO-tee.*

1321. Dark. Tmavý. *TMAH-vee.*

1322. Light. Světlý. *SVYĚT-lee.*

1323. Medium. Středního odstínu.
STRZHĚD-n^yee-haw AWT-st^yee-noo.

MATERIALS
HMOTY

1324. Metal. Kov. *kawf.*

1325. Aluminium. Hliník (OR: Aluminium).
HLĬ-n^yeek (OR: *AH-loo-mee-nĭ-yoom*).

1326. Brass. Mosaz. *MAW-sahs.*

1327. Copper. Měď. *mn^yĕt^y.*

1328. Gold. Zlato. *ZLAH-taw.*

1329. Silver. Stříbro. *STRZHEEB-raw.*

1330. Textiles. Textilie. *TĚKS-tee-lĭ-yĕ.*

1331. Cotton. Bavlna. *BAH-vŭl-nah.*

1332. Silk. Hedvábí. *HĚD-vah-bee.*

1333. Synthetic fabrics. Umělá vlákna.
OO-mnʸĕ-lāh VLĀHK-nah.

1334. Orlon. Orlon. *AWR-lawn.*

1335. Nylon. Nylon. *NAH‿Y-lawn.*

1336. Silon (a Czech synthetic fabric). Silon.
SĬ-lawn.

1337. Wool. Vlna. *VŬL-nah.*

1338. Ceramic. Keramika. *KĚ-rah-mĭ-kah.*

1339. China. (Jemný) porculán.
(YĔM-neͤ) PAWR-tsoo-lāhn.

1340. Glass. Sklo. *sklaw.*

1341. Lace. Krajkovina (OR: Krajka).
KRAH‿Y-kaw-vĭ-nah (OR: KRAH‿Y-kah).

1342. Leather. Kůže. *KŌŌ-zhĕ.*

1343. Plastic. Plastická (OR: Umělá) hmota.
PLAHS-tĭts-kāh (OR: OO-mnʸĕ-lāh) HMAW-tah.

1344. Porcelain. Porculán. *PAWR-tsoo-lāhn.*

1345. Stone. Kámen. *KĀH-mĕn.*

1346. Stoneware. Kamenina. *KAH-mĕ-nʸĭ-nah.*

1347. Wood. Dřevo. *DRZHĔ-vaw.*

BOOKSHOP, STATIONER, NEWSDEALER
KNIHKUPECTVÍ, PAPÍRNICTVÍ, NOVINOVÝ STÁNEK

1348. Playing cards. Hrací karty.
HRAH-tsee KAHR-tĭ.

1349. A dictionary. Slovník. *SLAWV-nᵛeek.*

1350. A dozen envelopes. Tucet obálek.
TOO-tsĕt AW-bah-lĕk.

1351. An eraser. Guma na vymazování.
GOO-mah NAH-vĭ-mah-zaw-vah-nᵛee.

1352. Fiction. Románová literatura.
RAW-mah-naw-vah LĬ-tĕ-rah-too-rah.

1353. Folders. Desky na listiny.
DĔS-kĭ NAH-lĭs-tᵛĭ-nĭ.

1354. A guide book. Průvodce. *PROO-vawt-tsĕ.*

1355. Ink. Inkoust. *ĬN-koh‿oost.*

1356. A map. Mapa. *MAH-pah.*

1357. Some magazines. Nějaké časopisy.
NᵛĔ-yah-keh CHAH-saw-pĭ-sĭ.

1358. A newspaper. Noviny. *NAW-vĭ-nĭ.*

1359. Nonfiction. Poučná literatura.
PAW-ooch-nah LĬ-tĕ-rah-too-rah.

1360. **A notebook.** Zápisník. *ZĀH-pĭs-nʸeek.*

1361. **A small notebook.** Zápisníček.
ZĀH-pĭs-nʸee-chĕk.

1362. **Carbon paper.** Uhlový (OR: Karbonový) papír.
OO-hlaw-vee (OR: *KAHR-baw-naw-vee*) *PAH-peer.*

1363. **Onionskin paper.**
Letecký (OR: Průklepový) papír.
LĔ-tĕts-kee (OR: *PROO-klĕ-paw-vee*) *PAH-peer.*

1364. **Writing paper.** Psací papír.
PSAH-tsee PAH-peer.

1365. **Fountain pen.** Plnicí pero.
PŬL-nʸĭ-tsee PĔ-raw.

1366. **Ballpoint pen.** Kuličkové pero.
KOO-lĭch-kaw-veh PĔ-raw.

1367. **A pencil.** Tužka. *TOOSH-kah.*

1368. **Postcards.** Korespondenční lístky.
KAW-rĕs-pawn-dĕnch-nʸee LEEST-kĭ.

1369. **Picture postcards.** Pohlednice.
PAW-hlĕd-nʸĭ-tsĕ.

1370. **A roll of string.** Klubko provázku.
KLOOP-kaw PRAW-vahs-koo.

1371. **Tape.** Lepicí páska. *LĔ-pĭ-tsee PĀHS-kah.*

1372. **Scotch tape.** Průhledná lepicí páska.
PROO-hlĕd-nah LĔ-pĭ-tsee PĀHS-kah.

1373. **String.** Provázek (OR: Motouz).
  PRAW-vah-zěk (OR: *MAW-toh͝-oos*).

1374. **A typewriter.** Psací stroj. *PSAH-tsee stroy*.

1375. **Typewriter ribbon.** Páska do psacího stroje.
  PAHS-kah DAW-psah-tsee-haw STRAW-yě.

1376. **Wrapping paper.** Balicí papír.
  BAH-lǐ-tsee PAH-peer.

PHARMACY
LÉKÁRNA

1377. **Is there [a pharmacy] here where they understand English?**
  Je tu [nějaká lékárna], kde se dorozumím anglicky?
  yě too [NʸĚ-yah-kah LĚH-kahr-nah], GDĚ-sě DAW-raw-zoo-meem AHN-glǐts-kǐ?

1378. **May I speak [to a male clerk]?**
  Mohl bych mluvit [s prodavačem]?
  MAW-hǔl-bǐkh MLOO-vǐt [SPRAW-dah-vah-chěm]?

1379. **— to a female clerk.** — s prodavačkou.
  — SPRAW-dah-vahch-koh͝-oo.

**1380. Can you fill this prescription immedi-
ately?**

Můžete mi vyhotovit tento předpis ihned?

*MŌŌ-zhě-tě mǐ VĬ-haw-taw-vǐt TĚN-taw
PRZHĚT-pǐs Ĭ-hnět?*

1381. Can you refill this prescription?

Můžete mi znovu vyhotovit tento předpis?

*MŌŌ-zhě-tě mǐ ZNAW-voo VĬ-haw-taw-vǐt
TĚN-taw PRZHĚT-pǐs?*

1382. Is it mild?

Je to mírný prostředek?

yě taw MĒĒR-nee PRAW-strzhě-děk?

1383. Is it safe?

Je to bezpečný prostředek?

yě taw BĚS-pěch-nee PRAW-strzhě-děk?

1384. Caution.

Pozor!

PAW-zawr!

1385. Poison.

Jed.

yět.

1386. Take as directed.

Používejte, jak předepsáno.

*PAW-oo-zhee-vay-tě, yahk PRZHĚ-dě-psah-
naw.*

1387. Not to be taken internally (LIT.: **Do not swallow; only for external use**).

Nepožívat! Jen k vnějšímu použití.

NĚ-paw-zhee-vaht! yěn KVNᵞAY-shee-moo PAW-oo-zhĭ-tᵞee.

1388. To be taken according to [the doctor's] directions.

Používejte podle pokynů [lékaře].

PAW-oo-zhee-vay-tě PAW-dlě PAW-kĭ-noo [LEH-kah-rzhě].

See also "Health and Illness," p. 185.

DRUG STORE ITEMS
DROGISTICKÉ ZBOŽÍ

1389. Adhesive tape. Náplasťová páska.
NAH-plahs-tᵞaw-vah PAHS-kah.

1390. Analgesic (aspirin). Aspirín. *AHS-pĭ-reen.*

1391. Alcohol. Líh. *leekh.*

1392. Antiseptic. Dezinfekční prostředek.
DĚZ-ĭn-fěkch-nᵞee PRAW-strzhě-děk.

1393. Band aids. Náplast. *NAH-plahst.*

1394. Bandages. Obvazy. *AWB-vah-zĭ.*

1395. Bath oil. Koupelový olej.
   KOH‿OO-pĕ-law-vee AW-lay.

1396. Bath salts. Koupelová sůl.
   KOH‿OO-pĕ-law-vah sool.

1397. Bicarbonate of soda. Jedlá soda.
   YĔD-lah SAW-dah.

1398. Bobby pins. Vlásničky. *VLAHS-nʸĭch-kĭ.*

1399. Boric acid. Bórová kyselina.
   BAW-raw-vah KĬ-sĕ-lĭ-nah.

1400. Chewing gum. Žvýkací guma (OR: Žvýkačka).
   ZHVEE-kah-tsee GOO-mah (OR: ZHVEE-kahch-kah).

1401. Cleaning fluid. Čisticí prostředek.
   CHIS-tʸĭ-tsee PRAW-str zhĕ-dĕk.

1402. Cleansing tissues. Kosmetický papír.
   KAWS-mĕ-tĭts-kee PAH-peer.

1403. Cold cream. Studený krém. *STOO-dĕ-nee krehm.*

1404. Cologne. Kolínská voda.
   KAW-leen-skah VAW-dah.

1405. Comb. Hřeben. *HRZHĔ-bĕn.*

1406. Compact. Pudřenka. *POOD-rzhĕn-kah.*

1407. Contraceptives. Kontracepční prostředky.
   KAWN-trah-tsĕp-chnʸee PRAW-str zhĕt-kĭ.

1408. Corn pad. Náplast na kuří oka.
   NAH-plahst NAH-koo-rzhee AW-kah.

1409. Cotton (absorbent). Vata. *VAH-tah.*

1410. Cough syrup. Syrup proti kašli.
SĬ-roop PRAW-t^{y}ĭ KAHSH-lĭ.

1411. Deodorant. Deodorant. *DĚ-aw-daw-rahnt.*

1412. Depilatory. Prostředek k odstranění chloupků.
PRAW-strzhě-děk   KAWT-strah-n^{y}ě-n^{y}ee KHLOH_OOP-k$\overline{oo}$.

1413. Disinfectant. Dezinfekční prostředek.
DEZ-ĭn-fěkch-n^{y}ee PRAW-strzhě-děk.

1414. Ear plugs. Zátky do uší.
ZĀHT-kĭ DAW-oo-shee.

1415. Enema bag. Klystýrový vak.
KLĬ-stee-raw-vee vahk.

1416. Epsom salts. Hořká sůl. *HAWRZH-k$\overline{ah}$ sool.*

1417. Eye cup. Oční baňka.
AWCH-n^{y}ee BAHN^y-kah.

1418. Eye wash. Roztok k vymývání očí.
RAWS-tawk KVĬ-mee-v$\overline{ah}$-n^{y}ee AW-chee.

1419. Gauze. Gáza. *G$\overline{AH}$-zah.*

1420. Hairbrush. Kartáč na vlasy.
KAHR-t$\overline{ah}$chs NAH-vlah-sĭ.

1421. Hair clip. Spona do vlasů.
SPAW-nah DAW-vlah-soo.

1422. Hair tonic. Prostředek na vlasy.
PRAW-strzhě-děk NAH-vlah-sĭ.

1423. Hair net. Síťka na vlasy.
$\overline{SEET}$ʸ-kah NAH-vlah-sĭ.

1424. Hair pins. Vlásničky. $VL\overline{AH}S$-nʸĭch-kĭ.

1425. Hair spray. Lak na vlasy.
lahk NAH-vlah-sĭ.

1426. Hand lotion. (Tekutý) krém na ruce.
($T\breve{E}$-koo-$\overline{tee}$) kre$\overline{h}$m NAH-roo-tsĕ.

1427. Hot water bottle. Zahřívací láhev.
ZAH-hrzhe͞e-vah-tsee $L\overline{AH}$-hĕf.

1428. Ice bag. (Plastický) pytlík na ledový obklad.
($PLAHS$-tĭts-ke͞e) $P\breve{I}T$-le͞ek NAH-lĕ-daw-ve͞e
AWP-klaht.

1429. Insecticide. Prostředek proti hmyzu.
PRAW-strzhĕ-dĕk PRAW-tʸĭ HM$\breve{I}$-zoo.

1430. Iodine. Jódová tinktura.
$Y\overline{AW}$-daw-$\overline{vah}$ T$\breve{I}$NK-$\overline{too}$-rah.

1431. [Mild] laxative. [Mírné] projímadlo.
[$\overline{MEER}$-ne͞eh] PRAW-ye͞e-mahd-law.

1432. Lipstick. Rtěnka. RTʸ$\breve{E}$N-kah.

1433. Medicine dropper. Kapátko.
$K\acute{A}H$-pa͞eht-kaw.

1434. Mirror. Zrcátko. Z$\overline{U}$R-tsaht-kaw.

1435. Mouth wash. Ústní voda.
$\overline{OO}ST$-nʸe͞e VAW-dah.

1436. Nail file. Pilníček na nehty.
P$\breve{I}$L-nʸe͞e-chĕk NA-nĕkh-tĭ.

1437. Nail polish. Lak na nehty. *lahk NAH-někh-tĭ.*

1438. Nose drops. Kapky do nosu.
KAHP-kĭ DAW-naw-soo.

1439. Ointment. Mast. *mahst.*

1440. Pacifier. Dětské šidítko (OR: Dudlík).
DᵘĚT-skeh SHĬ-dᵘeet-kaw (OR: *DOOD-leek*).

1441. Peroxide. Kysličník vodičitý.
KĬS-lĭch-nᵘeek VAW-dᵘĭ-chĭ-tee.

1442. Pin. Špendlík. *SHPĚND-leek.*

1443. Powder. Zásyp. *ZAH-sĭp.*

1444. Face powder. Pudr. *POO-dŭr.*

1445. Foot powder. Prášek proti pocení nohou.
*PRAH-shĕk PRAW-tᵘĭ PAW-tsĕ-nᵘee NAW-
hoh‿oo.*

1446. Talcum powder. Steatitový prášek.
STĚ-ah-tĭ-taw-vee PRAH-shĕk.

1447. Powder puff. Labutěnka (OR: Pudrovátko).
LAH-boo-tᵘĕn-kah (OR: *POOD-raw-vaht-kaw*).

1448. Straight razor. Břitva. *BRZHĬT-vah.*

1449. Electric razor. Elektrický holicí strojek.
Ě-lĕk-trĭts-kee HAW-lĭ-tsee STRAW-yĕk.

1450. Safety razor. Holicí strojek.
HAW-lĭ-tsee STRAW-yĕk.

1451. Razor blade. Holicí čepelka.
HAW-lĭ-tsee CHĚ-pĕl-kah.

1452. Rouge. Šminka. *SHMĬN-kah.*

1453. Safety pin. Zapínací špendlík.
ZAH-pēe-nah-tsee SHPĔND-lēek.

1454. Sanitary napkins. Dámské (měsíční) vložky.
D̄AHM-skēh (MN^{y}Ĕ-seech-n^{y}ee) VLAWSH-kĭ.

1455. Scissors. Nůžky. *N̄OOSH-kĭ.*

1456. Seasickness remedy.
Prostředek proti mořské nemoci.
*PRAW-strzhĕ-dĕk PRAW-t^{y}ĭ MAWRZH-skĕh
NĔ-maw-tsĭ.*

1457. Sedative. Utišující prostředek.
OO-t^{y}ĭ-shoo-yee-tsee PRAW-strzhĕ-dĕk.

1458. Shampoo. Šampon. *SHAM-pawn.*

1459. [Brushless] shaving cream.
Holicí krém [pro nanášení bez štětky].
*HAW-lĭ-tsee krēhm [PRAW-nah-nah-shĕ-n^{y}ee
BĔS-sht^{y}ĕt-kĭ].*

1460. Shaving lotion. Vodička po holení.
VAW-d^{y}ĭch-kah PAW-haw-lĕ-n^{y}ee.

1461. Shaving brush. Holicí štětka.
HAW-lĭ-tsee SHT^{y}ĔT-kah.

1462. Shower cap. Čapka do sprchy.
CHAHP-kah DAW-spŭr-khĭ.

1463. Smelling salts. Vonná sůl. *VAWN-nah sool.*

1464. Soap. Mýdlo. *M̄EED-law.*

1465. Sponge. Houba. *HOH‿OO-bah.*

1466. Sunburn ointment. Krém proti úžehu.
krehm PRAW-t^{y}ĭ $\overline{OO}$-zhĕ-hoo.

1467. Sunglasses. Brýle proti slunci.
$\overline{BREE}$-lĕ PRAW-t^{y}ĭ SLOON-tsĭ.

1468. Suntan oil. Olej na opalování.
AW-lay NAH-aw-pah-law-vah-n^{y}ee.

1469. Syringe. Stříkačka. *STRZH$\overline{EE}$-kahch-kah.*

1470. [Centigrade] Fahrenheit thermometer.
Teploměr [s Celsiovou stupnicí] s Fahrenheito-
vou stupnicí.
*TĔP-law-mn^{y}ĕr [STSĔL-sĭ-yaw-voh‿oo STOOP-
n^{y}ĭ-tsee] SFAH-rĕn-hah‿y-taw-voh‿oo STOOP-
n^{y}ĭ-tsee.*

1471. Toothbrush. Kartáček na zuby.
KAHR-tah-chĕk NAH-zoo-bĭ.

1472. Toothpaste. Zubní pasta.
ZOOB-n^{y}ee PAHS-tah.

1473. Toothpowder. Zubní prášek.
ZOOB-n^{y}ee PR$\overline{AH}$-shĕk.

1474. Vaseline. Vazelína. *VAH-zĕ-$\overline{lee}$-nah.*

1475. Vitamins. Vitamíny. *VĬ-tah-$\overline{mee}$-nĭ.*

1476. Washcloth. Žínka. *ZH$\overline{EE}$N-kah.*

CAMERA SHOP AND PHOTOS

OBCHOD S FOTOGRAFICKÝMI POTŘEBAMI A FOTOGRA-FOVÁNÍ

1477. **I want (a roll of) film for this camera.**
Chci film do tohoto aparátu.
khtsĭ film DAW-taw-haw-taw AH-pah-rah-too.

1478. **Do you have [color film]?**
Máte [barevný film]?
MAH-tĕ [BAH-rĕv-nee film]?

1479. **— black and white film.** — černobílý film.
— CHĔR-naw-bee-lee film.

1480. **What is the charge [for developing a roll]?**
Kolik stojí [vyvolání jednoho filmu]?
KAW-lĭk STAW-yee [VĬ-vaw-lah-nʸee YĔD-naw-haw FĬL-moo]?

1481. **— for enlarging.** — zvětšeniny.
— ZVYĔT-shĕ-nʸĭ-nĭ.

1482. **— for one print.** — jedna kopie.
— YĔD-nah KAW-pĭ-yĕ.

1483. **May I take a photo of you?**
Mohu vás vyfotografovat?
MAW-hoo vahs VĬ-faw-taw-grah-faw-vaht?

1484. Would you take a photo of me, please?
Prosím vás, vyfotografoval byste mě?
*PRAW-seem vahs, VĬ-faw-taw-grah-faw-vahl
BĬS-těh mnᵘě?*

1485. A color print.
Barevná kopie.
BAH-rěv-nah KAW-pĭ-yě.

1486. Flashbulbs.
Žárovky pro bleskové světlo.
*ZHĀH-rawf-kĭ PRAW-blěs-kaw-věh SVYĚT-
law.*

1487. The lens.
Čočka.
CHAWCH-kah.

1488. Movie film.
Kinofilm.
KĬ-naw-fĭlm.

1489. The negative.
Negativ.
NĚ-gah-teef.

1490. The shutter.
Závěrka.
ZĀH-vyěr-kah.

1491. A transparency.
Diapozitiv.
DĬ-yah-paw-zĭ-teef.

1492. A tripod.
Podstavec.
PAWT-stah-věts.

See also "Repairs and Adjustments," p. 173.

GIFT AND SOUVENIR SHOP
OBCHOD S DÁRKOVÝM A PAMÁTKOVÝM ZBOŽÍM

1493. Ash tray. Popelníček. *PAW-pĕl-nʸee-chĕk.*

1494. Basket. Košík. *KAW-sheek.*

1495. Box of candy. Bonboniéra.
BAWN-baw-nĭ-yeh-rah.

1496. Doll. Panna. *PAHN-nah.*

1497. Embroidery (OR: **Needlework**). Výšivka.
VEE-shĭf-kah.

1498. Handicrafts. Ruční práce.
ROOCH-nʸee PRAH-tsĕ.

1499. Jewelry. Klenoty. *KLĔ-naw-tĭ.*

1500. Lace. Krajka. *KRAH‿Y-kah.*

1501. Penknife. Kapesní nůž.
KAH-pĕs-nʸee noosh.

1502. **Perfume.** Parfém. *PAHR-fĕhm.*

1503. **Phonograph records.** Gramofonové desky.
GRAH-maw-faw-naw-vēh DĔS-kĭ.

1504. **Precious stone.** Drahokam. *DRAH-haw-kahm.*

1505. **Reproduction (of painting, etc.).** Kopie.
KAW-pĭ-yĕ.

1506. **Souvenir.** Upomínkový předmět.
OO-paw-meen-kaw-vee PRZHĔD-mnᵛĕt.

1507. **Toys.** Hračky. *HRAHCH-kĭ.*

1508. **Vase.** Váza. *VĀH-zah.*

CIGAR STORE
TRAFIKA

1509. **Where is the nearest cigar store?**
Kde je tu nejbližší trafika?
gdĕ yĕ too NAY-blĭsh-shee TRAH-fĭ-kah?

1510. **I want some cigars.**
Chtěl bych nějaké doutníky.
KHTᵛĔL-bĭkh NᵛĔ-yah-keh DOH_OOT-nᵛee-kĭ.

1511. **A pack of cigarettes, please.**
Prosil bych krabičku cigaret.
PRAW-sĭl-bĭkh KRAH-bĭch-koo TSĬ-gah-rĕt.

1512. I need a lighter.
Potřebuji zapalovač.
PAW-trzhě-boo-yĭ ZAH-pah-law-vahch.

1513. Flint.
Kamínek do zapalovače.
KAH-mee-něk DAW-zah-pah-law-vah-chě.

1514. Lighter fluid.
Benzín do zapalovače.
BEN-zeen DAW-zah-pah-law-vah-chě.

1515. Matches.
Zápalky.
ZAH-pahl-kĭ.

1516. A pipe.
Dýmka.
DEEM-kah.

1517. Pipe tobacco.
Dýmkový tabák.
DEEM-kaw-vee TAH-bahk.

1518. A pouch.
Váček na tabák.
VAH-chěk NAH-tah-bahk.

LAUNDRY AND DRY CLEANING

PRÁDELNA A CHEMICKÁ ČISTÍRNA

1519. Where can I take my laundry to be cleaned?

Kde si mohu dát vyprat prádlo?

GDĚ-sĭ MAW-hoo daht VĬ-praht PRĀHD-law?

1520. Is there a dry-cleaning service near here?

Je zde nablízku chemická čistírna oděvů?

yě zdě NAH-blees-koo KHĚ-mĭts-kah CHĬS-tⁱ͡eer-nah AW-dʸě-voo?

1521. Wash this blouse [in hot water].

Vyperte mi tuto halenku [v horké vodě].

VĬ-pěr-tě mĭ TOO-taw HAH-lěn-koo [VHAWR-keh VAW-dʸě].

1522. — in warm water. — v teplé vodě.

— FTĚP-leh VAW-dʸě.

1523. — in lukewarm water.

— ve vlažné vodě.

— VĚ-vlahzh-neh VAW-dʸě.

1524. **— in cold water.** — ve studené vodě.
— *VĚ-stoo-dě-neh VAW-dʸě.*

1525. **No starch, please.**
Neškrobit, prosím.
NĚ-shkraw-bĭt, PRAW-seem.

1526. **Do not wash [this shirt] in hot water.**
Neperte [tuto košili] v horké vodě.
NĚ-pĕr-tě [TOO-taw KAW-shĭ-lĭ] VHAWR-keh VAW-dʸě.

1527. **Remove this stain.**
Vyčistěte tuto skvrnu.
VĬ-chĭs-tʸě-tě TOO-taw SKVŬR-noo.

1528. **Press [the trousers].**
Vyžehlete mi [kalhoty].
VĬ-zhĕ-hlě-tě mĭ [KAHL-haw-tĭ].

1529. **Starch [the collar].**
Naškrobte [límeček].
NAH-shkrawp-tě [LĒE-mě-chěk].

1530. **Dry-clean [this coat].**
Vyčistěte mi [tento kabát].
VĬ-chĭs-tʸě-tě mĭ [TĚN-taw KAH-baht].

1531. **The belt is missing.**
Schází pásek.
SKHĀH-zee PĀH-sěk.

1532. **Sew on [this button].**
Přišijte [tento knoflík].
PRZHĬ-shee‿y-tě [TĚN-taw KNAWF-leek].

1533. **Sew [this tear].**
Zašijte [toto roztržené místo].
*ZAH-shee⌣y-tě [TAW-taw RAWS-tŭr-zhě-neh
MEES-taw].*

See also "Repairs and Adjustments," which
follows.

REPAIRS AND ADJUSTMENTS
OPRAVY A ÚPRAVY

1534. **This is not working [any more].**
Tohle [už] nefunguje.
TAW-hlě [oosh] NĚ-foon-goo-yě.

1535. **This watch [is fast] is slow.**
Tyto hodinky se [předbíhají] zpožďují.
*TǏ-taw HAW-dʸĭn-kĭ-sě PRZHĚD-bee-hah-
yee] SPAWZH-dʸoo-yee.*

1536. **[My glasses] are broken.**
Rozbily se mi [brýle].
RAWZ-bĭ-lĭ-sě mĭ [BREE-lě].

1537. **Where can I repair it?**
Kde si to mohu dát opravit?
GDĚ-sĭ taw MAW-hoo daht AW-prah-vĭt?

1538. Fix [this lock].
Opravte [tento zámek].
AW-prahf-tě [TĚN-taw ZÁH-měk].

1539. Repair [the sole].
Opravte [podešev].
AW-prahf-tě [PAW-dě-shěf].

1540. — the heel. — podpatek.
— *PAWT-pah-těk.*

1541. — the uppers. — svršky. **— *SVŮRSH-kĭ.***

1542. — the strap. — přezku. **— *PRZHĚS-koo.***

1543. Adjust [this hearing aid].
Seřiďte [tento aparát pro nedoslýchavé].
SĚ-rzhĭt ⁱ-tě [TĚN-taw AH-pah-raht PRAW-
ně-daw-slee-khah-veh].

1544. Lengthen [this skirt].
Prodlužte [tuto sukni].
PRAW-dloosh-tě [TOO-taw SOOK-nⁱĭ].

1545. Shorten [the sleeves].
Zkraťte [rukávy].
SKRAHT ⁱ-tě [ROO-kah-vĭ].

1546. Replace [the lining].
Vyměňte [podšívku].
VĬ-mnⁱěnⁱ-tě [PAWT-sheef-koo].

1547. Mend [the pocket].
Opravte [kapsu].
AW-prahf-tě [KAHP-soo].

1548. Fasten it together.
Sepněte to dohromady.
SĚ-pn^yě-tě taw DAW-hraw-mah-dĭ.

1549. Clean the mechanism.
Vyčistěte mechanismus.
VĬ-chĭs-t^yě-tě MĚ-khah-nĭz-moos.

1550. Lubricate [the spring].
Naolejujte [péro].
NAH-aw-lě-yoo‿y-tě [PĒH-raw].

1551. An alteration.
Úprava.
ŌŌ-prah-vah.

1552. Needle.
Jehla.
YĚ-hlah.

1553. Scissors.
Nůžky.
NŌŌSH-kĭ.

1534. Thimble.
Náprstek.
NĀH-pŭrs-těk.

1555. Thread.
Nit.
n^yĭt.

BARBER SHOP
HOLIČSTVÍ

1556. A haircut, please.
Stříhat, prosím.
STRZHEE-haht, PRAW-seem.

1557. A light trim, please.
Prosil bych trochu podstřihnout.
*PRAW-sĭl-bĭkh TRAW-khoo PAWT-strzhĭ-
hnoh_oot.*

1558. Don't cut too much [off the top].
Neberte mi příliš hodně vlasů [seshora].
*NĚ-běr-tě mĭ PRZHEE-lĭsh HAWD-nʸě
VLAH-soo [SĚ-skhaw-rah].*

1559. — on the sides. — po stranách.
— *PAW-strah-nahkh.*

1560. Keep it long.
Nechte to dlouhé.
NĚKH-tě taw DLOH_OO-heh.

1561. I part my hair [on this side].
Dělám si pěšinku [na této straně].
*DʸĚ-lahm-sĭ PYĚ-shĭn-koo [NAH-teh-taw
STRAH-nʸě].*

1562. — on the other side. — na druhé straně.
— *NAH-droo-heh STRAH-nʸě.*

1563. — **in the middle.** — uprostřed.
— *OO-praw-str zhĕt.*

1564. **No hair tonic.**
Nedávejte mi vodičku na vlasy.
*NĔ-dah-vay-tĕ mĭ VAW-dᵘĭch-koo NAH-vlah-
sĭ.*

1565. **Trim [my moustache].**
Zastřihněte mi trochu [knír].
ZAH-str zhĭ-hnᵘĕ-tĕ mĭ TRAW-khoo [knᵘ̄eer].

1566. — **my eyebrows.** — obočí.
— *AW-baw-chee.*

1567. **Shorten my beard.**
Zkraťte mi vousy.
SKRAHTᵘ-tĕ mĭ VOH‿OO-sĭ.

1568. **Leave my sideburns as they are.**
Nechte mi licousy, jak je mám.
NĔKH-tĕ mĭ LĬ-tsoh‿oo-sĭ, yahk yĕ mahm.

1569. **Scissors only, please.**
Prosím, pouze nůžkami.
PRAW-̄seem, POH‿OO-zĕ N̄OOSH-kah-mi.

1570. **A shave.**
Holení.
HAW-lĕ-nᵘee.

1571. **A shoeshine.**
Čištění obuvi.
CHĬSH-tᵘĕ-nᵘee AW-boo-vĭ.

BEAUTY PARLOR
KADEŘNICTVÍ

**1572. Can I make an appointment for two
P.M.?**
Mohu si zamluvit kadeřnici na dvě hodiny
odpoledne?
*MAW-hoo-sĭ ZAH-mloo-vĭt KAH-děrzh-nʸĭ-
tsĭ NAH-dvyĕ HAW-dʸĭ-nĭ AWT-paw-lĕd-
nĕ?*

1573. Wash my hair.
Umyjte mi vlasy.
OO-mee‿y-tĕ mĭ VLAH-sĭ.

1574. Not too short.
Ne příliš krátké.
NĔ-przhee-lĭsh KRĀHT-keh.

1575. In this style, please.
Tento účes, prosím.
TĔN-taw ŌŌ-chĕs, PRAW-seem.

1576. Don't change the style.
Neměňte účes.
NĔ-mnʸĕňʸ-tĕ ŌŌ-chĕs.

1577. Dye my hair [in this shade].
Zabarvěte mi vlasy [do tohoto odstínu].
*ZAH-bahr-vyĕ-tĕ mĭ VLAH-sĭ [DAW-taw-
haw-taw AWT-stʸee-noo].*

1578. A curl.
Kadeření.
KAH-dĕ-rzhĕ-nʸee.

1579. A facial.
Masáž obličeje.
MAH-sahsh AWB-lĭ-chĕ-yĕ.

1580. A hair set.
Natočení vlasů.
NAH-taw-chĕ-nʸee VLAH-soo.

1581. Hair tint.
Přeliv.
PRZHĚ-lĭf.

1582. A massage.
Masáž.
MAH-sahsh.

1583. A manicure.
Manikúra.
MAH-nĭ-koo-rah.

1584. A permanent wave.
Trvalá (ondulace).
TŬR-vah-lah (AWN-doo-lah-tsĕ).

1585. A set.
Natočení vlasů.
NAH-taw-chĕ-nʸee VLAH-soo.

1586. **A shampoo.**
Mytí vlasů.
MĬ-tᵞee VLAH-soo.

1587. **A wave.**
Ondulace.
AWN-doo-lah-tsě.

STORES AND SERVICES
OBCHODY A SLUŽBY

1588. **Antique shop.** Obchod se starožitnostmi.
AWP-khawt SĚ-stah-raw-zhĭt-nawst-mĭ.

1589. **Art gallery.** Výstavní síň.
VEE-stahv-nᵞee seenᵞ.

1590. **Artist's materials.** Potřeby pro umělce.
PAW-trzhě-bĭ PRAW-oo-mnᵞěl-tsě.

1591. **Auto rental.** Půjčovna aut.
POO‿Y-chawv-nah ah‿oot.

1592. **Auto repairs.** Opravy aut. *AW-prah-vĭ ah‿oot.*

1593. **Bakery.** Pekařství. *PĚ-kahr zhs-tvee.*

1594. **Bank.** Banka. *BAHN-kah.*

1595. **Bar.** Výčep lihovin. *VEE-chěp LĬ-haw-vĭn.*

1596. **Beauty salon.** Salón krásy.
SAH-lawn KRĀH-sĭ.

1597. **Bookshop.** Knihkupectví. *KN^{y}ĬKH-koo-pets-tvee̅.*

1598. **Butcher.** Řezník. *RZHĔZ-n^{y}ee̅k.*

1599. **Candy shop.** Cukrárna. *TSOOK-rah̅r-nah.*

1600. **Checkroom.** Šatna. *SHAHT-nah.*

1601. **Cigar store.** Trafika. *TRAH-fĭ-kah.*

1602. **Cinema (movie theater).** Kino (OR: Biograf).
KĬ-naw (OR: *BĬ-yaw-grahf*).

1603. **Cleaners and dyers.** Čistírna a barvírna.
CHĬS-t^{y}ee̅r-nah ah BAHR-vee̅r-nah.

1604. **Clothing store.** Obchod s konfekčním zbožím.
AWP-khawt SKAWN-fĕkch-n^{y}ee̅m ZBAW-zhee̅m.

1605. **Men's clothing.** Pánské oděvy.
PĀHN-ske̅h AW-d^{y}ĕ-vĭ.

1606. **Ladies' clothing.** Dámské oděvy.
DĀHM-ske̅h AW-d^{y}ĕ-vĭ.

1607. **Cosmetics.** Kosmetika. *KAWS-mĕ-tĭ-kah.*

1608. **Dance studio.** Taneční studio.
TAH-nĕch-n^{y}ee STŌŌ-dĭ-yaw.

1609. **Delicatessen.** Lahůdkařství.
LAH-hoo̅t-kahr zhs-tvee̅.

1610. **Dentist.** Zubní lékař. *ZOOB-n^{y}ee LĒH-kahrzh.*

1611. **Department store.** Jednotkový obchod.
YĔD-nawt-kaw-vee̅ AWP-khawt.

1612. **Dressmaker.** Dámská krejčová.
DĀHM-skah̅ KRAY-chaw-vah̅.

1613. Drug store. Drogerie. *DRAW-gĕ-rĭ-yĕ.*

1614. Electrical supplies. Elektrotechnické potřeby.
Ĕ-lĕk-traw-tĕkh-nĭts-kēh PAW-tr zhĕ-bĭ.

1615. Employment agency.
Zprostředkovatelna práce.
SPRAW-str zhĕt-kaw-vah-tĕl-nah PRĀH-tse.

1616. Florist. Květinářství. *KVYĔ-tʸi-nahr zhs-tvee.*

1617. Fruit store. Obchod s ovocem.
AWP-khawt SAW-vaw-tsĕm.

1618. Funeral parlor. Pohřební ústav.
PAW-hr zhĕb-nʸee ŌŌ-stahf.

1619. Furniture store. Obchod s nábytkem.
AWP-khawt SNĀH-bĭt-kĕm.

1620. Gift store. Obchod s dárkovým zbožím.
AWP-khawt ZDĀHR-kaw-veem ZBAW-zheem.

1621. Grocery store. Obchod s potravinami.
AWP-khawt SPAW-trah-vĭ-nah-mĭ.

1622. Ladies' hairdresser. Kadeřník.
KAH-dĕr zh-nʸeek.

1623. Men's hairdresser. Holič. *HAW-lĭch.*

1624. Hardware store. Železářství.
ZHĔ-lĕ-zahr zhs-tvee.

1625. Hat shop. Kloboučnictví.
KLAW-boh‿ooch-nʸĭts-tvee.

1626. **Housewares.** Potřeby pro domácnost.
   PAW-trzhĕ-bĭ PRAW-daw-mahts-nawst.

1627. **Jewelry store.** Klenotnictví.
   KLĔ-nawt-nʸĭts-tvee.

1628. **Lawyer.** Právník. *PRĀHV-nʸeek.*

1629. **Laundry and dry cleaner.**
   Prádelna a chemická čistírna.
   PRĀH-dĕl-nah   ah   KHĔ-mĭts-kāh   CHĬS-tʸeer-nah.

1630. **Loans.** Půjčky. *POO̱_YCH-kĭ.*

1631. **Lumberyard.** Sklad dřeva. *sklaht DRZHĔ-vah.*

1632. **Market.** Trh. *tŭrkh.*

1633. **Milliner.** Modistka. *MAW-dĭst-kah.*

1634. **Money exchange.** Směnárna peněz.
   SMNʸĔ-nahr-nah PĔ-nʸĕs.

1635. **Music store.** Obchod s hudebninami.
   AWP-khawt SKHOO-dĕb-nʸĭ-nah-mĭ.

1636. **Musical instruments.** Hudební nástroje.
   HOO-dĕb-nʸee NĀH-straw-yĕ.

1637. **Sheet music.** Hudebniny. *HOO-dĕb-nʸĭ-nĭ.*

1638. **Paints.** Barvy. *BAHR-vĭ.*

1639. **Pastry shop.** Cukrářství. *TSOOK-rahrzhs-tvee.*

1640. **Pet shop.** Obchod s domácími zvířaty.
   AWP-khawt ZDAW-mah-tsee-mĭ ZVEE-rzhah-tĭ.

1641. Pharmacy. Lékárna. *LEH-kahr-nah.*

1642. Photographer. Fotograf. *FAW-taw-grahf.*

1643. Post office. Pošta. *PAWSH-tah.*

1644. Printing (OR: **Print shop**). Tiskárna.
TʸĬS-kahr-nah.

1645. Radio. Rádio. *RAH-dĭ-yaw.*

1646. Real estate. Realitní kancelář.
RĔ-ah-lĭt-nʸee KAHN-tsĕ-lahrzh.

1647. Sewing machines. Šicí stroje.
SHĬ-tsee STRAW-yĕ.

1648. Shoemaker. Obuvník. *AW-boov-nʸeek.*

1649. Shoeshine. Čištění obuvi.
CHĬSH-tʸĕ-nʸee AW-boo-vĭ.

1650. Shoe store. Obchod s obuví.
AWP-khawt SAW-boo-vee.

1651. Shopping center. Obchodní středisko.
AWP-khawd-nʸee STRZHĔ-dʸĭs-kaw.

1652. Sightseeing. Prohlídka (města).
PRAW-hleet-kah (MNʸĔS-tah).

1653. Sign painter. Malíř štítů.
MAH-leerzh SHTʸEE-too.

1654. Sporting goods. Sportovní zboží.
SPAWR-tawv-nʸee ZBAW-zhee.

1655. Stockbroker. Burzovní maklér.
BOOR-zawv-nʸee MAHK-lehr.

1656. Supermarket.
Obchod s potravinami (se samoobsluhou).
*AWP-khawt SPAW-trah-vĭ-nah-mĭ (SĚ-sah-
maw-awp-sloo-hoh‿oo).*

1657. Tailor. Krejčí. *KRAY-chee.*

1658. Tobacco shop. Trafika. *TRAH-fĭ-kah.*

1659. Travel agent. Cestovní kancelář.
TSĚS-tawv-nʸee KAHN-tsě-lāhrzh.

1660. Trucking. Doprava nákladními auty.
DAW-prah-vah NĀH-klahd-nʸee-mĭ AH‿OO-tĭ.

1661. Upholsterer. Čalouník. *CHAH-loh‿oo-nʸeek.*

1662. Used cars. Oježděná auta.
AW-yĕzh-dʸĕ-nāh AH‿OO-tah.

1663. Vegetable store. Zelinářství.
ZĚ-lĭ-nāhrzhs-tvee.

1664. Watchmaker and repairs. Hodinářství.
HAW-dʸĭ-nāhrzhs-tvee.

1665. [Wines and] liquors. [Vína a] lihoviny.
[VEE-nah ah] LĬ-haw-vĭ-nĭ.

HEALTH AND ILLNESS
ZDRAVOTNÍ STAV

1666. Is the doctor [at home] in his office?
Je pan doktor [doma] v ordinaci?
*yě pahn DAWK-tawr [DAW-mah] VAWR-dĭ-
nah-tsĭ?*

1667. **What are his office hours** (LIT.: **When does the doctor give consultations**)?
Kdy ordinuje pan doktor?
gdĭ AWR-dĭ-noo-yĕ pahn DAWK-tawr?

1668. **I have something [in my eye].**
Mám něco [v oku].
mahm NʸĔ-tsaw [VAW-koo].

1669. **I have a pain [in my back].**
Bolí mě [v zádech].
BAW-lee mnʸĕ [VZĀH-dĕkh].

1670. **My [toe] is swollen.**
Mám oteklý [prst u nohy].
mahm AW-tĕk-lee [pŭrst OO-naw-hĭ].

1671. **It is sensitive to pressure.**
Je to citlivé na tlak.
yĕ taw TSĬT-lĭ-veh NAH-tlahk.

1672. **Is it serious?**
Je to vážné?
yĕ taw VĀHZH-neh?

1673. **I sleep poorly.**
Spím špatně.
speem SHPAHT-nʸĕ.

1674. **Can you give me something to relieve the pain?**
Můžete mi dát něco na zmírnění bolesti?
MOO-zhĕ-tĕ mĭ daht NʸĔ-tsaw NAH-zmeer-nʸĕ-nʸee BAW-les-tʸi?

1675. What shall I do?
Co mám dělat?
tsaw mãhm D^yĚ-laht?

1676. Do I have to go [to a hospital]?
Musím jít [do nemocnice]?
MOO-seem yeet [DAW-ně-mawts-n^yĭ-tsě]?

1677. Must I stay in bed?
Musím zůstat v posteli?
MOO-seem ZOO-staht FPAW-stě-lĭ?

1678. Is it contagious?
Je to nakažlivé?
yě taw NAH-kahzh-lĭ-veh?

1679. I feel [better] worse.
Cítím se [lépe] hůře.
TSEE-t^yeem-se [LEH-pě] HOO-rzhě.

1680. The condition has not improved.
Stav se nezlepšil.
STAHF-sě NĚ-zlěp-shĭl.

1681. Shall I keep it bandaged?
Mám to nechat obvázáno?
mãhm taw NĚ-khaht AWB-vah-zah-naw?

1682. Can I travel [Monday]?
Mohu cestovat [v pondělí]?
MAW-hoo TSĚS-taw-vaht [FPAWN-d^yě-lee]?

1683. When will you come again?
Kdy opět přijdete?
gdĭ AW-pyět PRZHEE_Y-dě-tě?

1684. **When should I take [the medicine]?**
Kdy mám brát [léky]?
gdǐ mahm braht [LEH-kǐ]?

1685. **— the injections. —** injekce.
— *ĬN-yĕk-tsĕ.*

1686. **— the pills. —** pilulky. — *PĬ-lool-kǐ.*

1687. **Every hour.**
Každou hodinu.
KAHZH-doh＿oo HAW-dᵘǐ-noo.

1688. **Before meals.**
Před jídlem.
PRZHĔD-yeed-lĕm.

1689. **After meals.**
Po jídle.
PAW-yeed-lĕ.

1690. **On going to bed.**
Před spaním.
PRZHĔT-spah-nᵘeem.

1691. **On getting up.**
Po probuzení.
PAW-praw-boo-zĕ-nᵘee.

1692. **Twice a day.**
Dvakrát denně.
DVAH-kraht DĔN-nᵘĕ.

1693. **An anesthetic.**
Anestetikum.
AH-nĕs-tĕ-tĭ-koom.

1694. **A drop.**
Kapka.
KAHP-kah.

1695. **An orthopedist.**
Ortopéd.
AWR-taw-pēht.

1696. **An oculist.**
Oční specialista.
AWCH-nʸee SPĚ-tsĭ-yah-lĭs-tah.

1697. **A specialist.**
Specialista.
SPĚ-tsĭ-yah-lĭs-tah.

1698. **A surgeon.**
Chirurg.
KHĬ-roork.

1699. **A teaspoonful.**
Kávová lžička.
KĀH-vaw-vāh LZHĬCH-kah.

1700. **X-ray.**
Rentgenový snímek.
RĚNT-gĕ-naw-vee SNʸEE-měk.

AILMENTS
NEMOCI

1701. **An allergy.** Alergie. *AH-lĕr-gĭ-yĕ.*

1702. An [acute] appendicitis attack.
[Akutní] zápal slepého střeva.
  [*AH-koot-n^{y}ee*] *ZAH-pahl   SLĚ-peh-haw
  STRZHĚ-vah.*

1703. An insect bite. Bodnutí hmyzem.
  BAWD-noo-t^{y}ee HMĬ-zěm.

1704. An abscess. Hnisavý nádor (OR: Vřed).
  HN^{y}Ĭ-sah-vee NAH-dawr (OR: *vrzhět*).

1705. A blister. Puchýř. *POO-kheerzh.*

1706. A boil. Vřídek. *VRZHEE-děk.*

1707. A burn. Spálenina. *SPAH-lě-n^{y}ĭ-nah.*

1708. Chicken pox. Plané neštovice.
  PLAH-neh NĚSH-taw-vĭ-tsě.

1709. A cold. Nachlazení. *NAH-khlah-zě-n^{y}ee.*

1710. A cut. Řezná rána. *RZHĚZ-nah RAH-nah.*

1711. Constipation. Zácpa. *ZAHTS-pah.*

1712. A cough. Kašel. *KAH-shěl.*

1713. A cramp. Křeč. *krzhěch.*

1716. Diarrhoea. Průjem. *PROO-yěm.*

1715. Dysentery. Úplavice. *OO-plah-vĭ-tsě.*

1716. An earache. Bolest v uších.
  BAW-lěst VOO-sheekh.

1717. A fever. Horečka. *HAW-rěch-kah.*

1718. Hay fever. Senná rýma. *SĚN-nah REE-mah.*

1719. A fracture. Zlomenina. *ZLAW-mě-n^yĭ-nah.*

1720. Headache. Bolení hlavy. *BAW-lě-n^yee HLAH-vĭ.*

1721. Indigestion. Špatné trávení.
SHPAHT-neh TRAH-vě-n^yee.

1722. Inflammation. Zápal (OR: Zanícení).
ZAH-pahl (OR: *ZAH-n^yee-tsě-n^yee*).

1723. Measles. Spalničky. *SPAHL-n^yĭch-kĭ.*

1724. German measles. Zarděnky. *ZAHR-d^yěn-kĭ.*

1725. Mumps. Příušnice. *PRZHEE-oosh-n^yĭ-tsě.*

1726. Nausea. Špatně od žaludku (OR: Nevolnost).
SHPAHT-n^yě AWD-zhah-loot-koo (OR: *NĚ-vawl-nawst*).

1727. Nosebleed. Krvácení nosu.
KŬR-vah-tsě-n^yee NAW-soo.

1728. Pneumonia. Zápal plic. *ZAH-pahl plĭts.*

1729. Poisoning. Otrava. *AW-trah-vah.*

1730. A sprain. Podvrtnutí. *PAWD-vŭrt-noo-t^yee.*

1731. A sore throat. Bolení v krku.
BAW-lě-n^yee FKŬR-koo.

1732. A sunburn. Úžeh (OR: Úpal).
OO-zhekh (OR: *OO-pahl*).

1733. A swelling. Otok. *AW-tawk.*

1734. Tonsillitis. Zánět mandlí (OR: Angína).
ZAH-n^yět MAHN-dlee (OR: *AHN-gee-nah*).

1735. Toothache. Bolení zubů.
    BAW-lĕ-n^{y}ee ZOO-b̄oo.

See also "Accidents," p. 194, "Parts of the Body," p. 195, and "Pharmacy," p. 157.

DENTIST
ZUBNÍ LÉKAŘ

1736. Do you know a good [dentist]?
    Znáte dobrého [zubního lékaře]?
    ZNĀH-tĕ DAWB-reh-haw [ZOOB-n^{y}ee-haw LĒH-kah-rzhĕ]?

1737. I have lost a filling (LIT.: **A filling of mine has fallen out**).
    Vypadla mi plomba.
    VĬ-pahd-lah mĭ PLAWM-bah.

1738. Can you fix [this filling]?
    Můžete mi opravit [tuto plombu]?
    MŌO-zhĕ-tĕ mĭ AW-prah-vĭt [TOO-taw PLAWM-boo]?

1739. — this bridge. — tento můstek.
    — *TĔN-taw MŌOS-tĕk.*

1740. — this denture. — tento umělý chrup.
    — *TĔN-taw OO-mn^{y}ĕ-lēe khroop.*

1741. [This molar] hurts me.
Bolí mě [tato stolička].
BAW-lee mnʸě [TAH-taw STAW-lĭch-kah].

1742. This front tooth.
Tento přední zub.
TĚN-taw PRZHĚD-nʸee zoop.

1743. This wisdom tooth.
Tento zub moudrosti.
TEN-taw zoop MOH͜OO-draws-tʸĭ.

1744. My gums are sore.
Bolí mě dásně.
BAW-lee mnʸě DĀHS-nʸě.

1745. I have a [broken tooth].
Mám [ulomený zub].
māhm [OO-law-mĕ-nee zoop].

1746. — an abscess. — hnisavý zánět.
— HNʸĬ-sah-vee ZĀH-nʸět.

1747. — a cavity. — děravý zub.
— DʸĚ-rah-vee zoop.

1748. Give me a [general] local anesthetic.
Dejte mi [celkovou] lokální anestézii.
DAY-tě mĭ [TSĚL-kaw-voh͜oo] LAW-kahl-nʸee AH-něs-teh-zĭ-yĭ.

1749. I do not want the tooth extracted.
Tento zub mi netrhejte.
TĚN-taw zoop mĭ NĚ-tŭr-hay-tě.

1750. **A temporary filling.**
Vložka.
VLAWSH-kah.

ACCIDENTS
NEHODY

1751. **There has been an accident.**
Došlo k nehodě.
DAW-shlaw KNĚ-haw-dʸĕ.

1752. **Call [a doctor] immediately.**
Rychle zavolejte [lékaře]. ___
RĬKH-lĕ ZAH-vaw-lay-tĕ [L͞E͞H-kah-rzhĕ].

1753. **— an ambulance.** — sanitku.
— SAH-nĭt-koo.

1754. **— a nurse.** — ošetřovatelku.
— AW-shĕt-rzhaw-vah-tĕl-koo.

1755. **— a policeman.** — Bezpečnost.
— BĔS-pĕch-nawst.

1756. **He has fallen.**
(On) upadl.
(awn) OO-pah-dŭl.

1757. **She has fainted.**
(Ona) omdlela.
(AW-nah) AWM-dlĕ-lah.

1758. He has a cut.
Má řeznou ránu.
mah RZHĔZ-noh‿oo RĀH-noo.

1759. [My finger] is bleeding.
Krvácí [mi prst].
KŬR-vah-tsee [mĭ pŭrst].

1760. A fracture [of the arm].
Zlomenina [ruky].
ZLAW-mĕ-nʸĭ-nah [ROO-kĭ].

1761. I want to [rest].
Chci si [odpočinout].
KHTSĬ-sĭ [AWT-paw-chĭ-noh‿oot].

1762. — sit down. — sednout. — *SĔD-noh‿oot.*

1763. — lie down. — lehnout. — *LĔ-hnoh‿oot.*

1764. Notify [my husband].
Podejte zprávu [mému manželovi].
PAW-day-tĕ SPRĀH-voo [MĒH-moo MAHN-zhĕ-law-vĭ].

1765. A tourniquet.
Turniket.
TOOR-nĭ-kĕt.

PARTS OF THE BODY
ČÁSTI LIDSKÉHO TĚLA

1766. Ankle. Kotník. *KAWT-nʸeek.*

1767. Appendix. Slepé střevo. *SLĚ-pȇh STRZHĚ-vaw.*

1768. Arm. Ruka (OR: Paže).
   ROO-kah (OR: *PAH-zhě*).

1769. Armpit. Podpaždí. *PAWT-pahzh-dᵞee.*

1770. Artery. Tepna. *TĚP-nah.*

1771. Back. Záda. *ZĀH-dah.*

1772. Beard. Vousy. *VOH‿OO-sĭ.*

1773. Belly. Břicho. *BRZHĬ-khaw.*

1774. Blood. Krev. *krĕf.*

1775. Blood vessel. Céva. *TSĒĒ-vah.*

1776. Bone. Kost. *kawst.*

1777. Brain. Mozek. *MAW-zĕk.*

1778. Breast. Prs (female); prsa (male).
   pŭrs; PŬR-sah.

1779. Calf. Lýtko. *LĒĒT-kaw.*

1780. Cheek. Tvář. *tvahrzh.*

1781. Chest. Prsa. *PŬR-sah.*

1782. Chin. Brada. *BRAH-dah.*

1783. Collarbone. Klíční kost. *KLĒĒCH-nᵞee kawst.*

1784. Ear. Ucho. *OO-khaw.*

1785. Elbow. Loket. *LAW-kĕt.*

1786. Eye. Oko. *AW-kaw.*

1787. Eyebrow. Obočí. *AW-baw-chee.*

1788. **Eyelashes.** Řasy. *RZHAH-sĭ.*

1789. **Eyelid.** Víčko. *VEECH-kaw.*

1790. **Face.** Obličej. *AWB-lĭ-chay.*

1791. **Finger.** Prst. *pŭrst.*

1792. **Fingernail.** Nehet. *NĔ-hĕt.*

1793. **Foot.** Noha. *NAW-hah.*

1794. **Forehead.** Čelo. *CHĔ-law.*

1795. **Gall bladder.** Žlučník. *ZHLOOCH-nʸeek.*

1796. **Genitals.** Pohlavní ústrojí.
      PAW-hlahv-nʸee OO-straw-yee.

1797. **Glands.** Žlázy. *ZHLAH-zĭ.*

1798. **Gums.** Dásně. *DAHS-nʸĕ.*

1799. **Hair.** Vlasy. *VLAH-sĭ.*

1800. **Hand.** Ruka. *ROO-kah.*

1801. **Head.** Hlava. *HLAH-vah.*

1802. **Heart.** Srdce. *SŬRT-tse.*

1803. **Heel.** Pata. *PAH-tah.*

1804. **Hip.** Kyčel (OR: Bok). *KĬ-chĕl* (OR: *bawk*).

1805. **Intestines.** Střeva. *STRZHĔ-vah.*

1806. **Jaw.** Čelist. *CHĔ-lĭst.*

1807. **Joint.** Kloub. *kloh‿oop.*

1808. **Kidneys.** Ledviny. *LĔD-vĭ-nĭ.*

1809. **Knee.** Koleno. *KAW-lĕ-naw.*

1810. **Larynx.** Hrtan. *HŬR-tahn.*

1811. **Leg.** Noha. *NAW-hah.*

1812. **Lip.** Ret. *rĕt.*

1813. **Liver.** Játra. *YĀH-trah.*

1814. **Lungs.** Plíce. *PLĒE-tsĕ.*

1815. **Mouth.** Ústa. *ŌOS-tah.*

1816. **Muscle.** Sval. *svahl.*

1817. **Nail.** Nehet. *NĔ-hĕt.*

1818. **Navel.** Pupek. *POO-pĕk.*

1819. **Neck.** Krk. *kŭrk.*

1820. **Nerve.** Nerv. *nĕrf.*

1821. **Nose.** Nos. *naws.*

1822. **Pancreas.** Slinivka břišní.
    SLĬ-nʸĭf-kah BRZHĬSH-nʸee.

1823. **Rib.** Žebro. *ZHĔB-raw.*

1824. **Shoulder.** Rameno. *RAH-mĕ-naw.*

1825. **Side.** Bok. *bawk.*

1826. **Skin.** Kůže. *KŌO-zhĕ.*

1827. **Skull.** Lebka. *LĔP-kah.*

1828. **Spine.** Páteř. *PĀH-tĕrzh.*

1829. **Spleen.** Slezina. *SLĔ-zĭ-nah.*

1830. **Stomach.** Žaludek. *ZHAH-loo-dĕk.*

1831. **Temple.** Spánek. *SPĀH-nĕk.*

1832. **Thigh.** Stehno. *STĚ-hnaw.*

1833. **Throat.** Krk (OR: Hrdlo).
    kŭrk (OR: *HŬRD-law*).

1834. **Thumb.** Palec. *PAH-lĕts.*

1835. **Toe.** Prst u nohy. *pŭrst OO-naw-hĭ.*

1836. **Tongue.** Jazyk. *YAH-zĭk.*

1837. **Tonsils.** Mandle. *MAHND-lĕ.*

1838. **[Tooth] teeth.** [Zub] zuby. [*zoop*] *ZOO-bĭ.*

1839. **Vein.** Žíla. *ZHEE-lah.*

1840. **Waist.** Pás. *pahs.*

1841. **Wrist.** Zápěstí. *ZAH-pyĕs-tᵛee.*

TIME
ČAS

1842. **What time is it?**
    Kolik je hodin?
    KAW-lĭk yĕ HAW-dᵛĭn?

1843. **[It is] early.**
    [Je] brzy.
    [*ye*] *BŬR-zĭ.*

1844. **[It is] late.**
    [Je] pozdě.
    [*yĕ*] *PAWZ-dᵛĕ.*

1845. Two A.M.
Dvě hodiny ráno.
dvyě HAW-d^{y}ĭ-nĭ R̄ĀH-naw.

1846. Two P.M.
Dvě hodiny odpoledne.
dvyě HAW-d^{y}ĭ-nĭ AWT-paw-lĕd-ně.

1847. Half-past three (LIT.: **Half of four**).
Půl čtvrté.
p̄ool CHTVŬR-teh.

1848. Quarter past four (LIT.: **Quarter to-ward five**).
Čtvrt na pět.
chtvŭrt NAH-pyět.

1849. Quarter to five (LIT.: **Three quarters toward five**).
Tři čtvrti na pět.
trzhĭ CHTVŬR-t^{y}ĭ NAH-pyět.

1850. Ten minutes to six (LIT.: **After ten minutes, six**).
Za deset minut šest.
ZAH-dě-sět MĬ-noot shěst.

1851. Twenty minutes past seven (LIT.: **After ten minutes, half of eight**).
Za deset minut půl osmé.
ZAH-dě-sět MĬ-noot p̄ool AWS-meh.

1852. In the morning.
Ráno.
RA͞H-naw.

1853. In the afternoon.
Odpoledne.
AWT-paw-lĕd-nĕ.

1854. In the evening.
Večer.
VĚ-chĕr.

1855. At noon.
V poledne.
FPAW-lĕd-nĕ.

1856. Midnight.
Půlnoc.
PO͞OL-nawts.

1857. The day.
Den.
dĕn.

1858. The night.
Noc.
nawts.

1859. Last night.
Včera v noci (OR: Včera večer).
FCHĚ-rah VNAW-tsĭ (OR: FCHĚ-rah VĚ-chĕr).

1860. Yesterday.
Včera.
FCHĚ-rah.

1861. Today.
Dnes.
dněs.

1862. Tonight.
Dnes v noci (OR: Dnes večer).
dněs VNAW-tsĭ (OR: *dněs VĔ-chĕr*).

1863. Tomorrow.
Zítra.
ZĒĒT-rah.

1864. Last month.
Minulý měsíc.
MĬ-noo-lēē MNᵘĔ-seets.

1865. Last year.
Loni.
LAW-nᵘĭ.

1866. Next Sunday.
Příští neděli.
PRZHĒĒSH-tᵘee NĔ-dᵘĕ-lĭ.

1867. Next week.
Příští týden.
PRZHĒĒSH-tᵘee TĒĒ-děn.

1868. The day before yesterday.
Předevčírem.
PRZHĔ-dĕ-ʃchee-rĕm.

1869. **The day after tomorrow.**
Pozítří.
PAW-zeet-rzhee.

1870. **Two weeks ago.**
Přede dvěma týdny.
PRZHĚ-dě DVYĚ-mah TEED-nǐ.

WEATHER
POČASÍ

1871. **How is it (the weather) today?**
Jak je dnes?
yahk yě dněs?

1872. **Cold.**
Chladno.
KHLAHD-naw.

1873. **Fair.**
Dost hezky.
dawst HĚS-kǐ.

1874. **[Very] warm.**
[Velmi] teplo.
[VĚL-mǐ] TĚP-law.

1875. **Hot.**
Horko.
HAWR-kaw.

1876. Beautiful.
Překrásně.
PRZHĚ-krahs-nᵘĕ.

1877. It is sunny.
Je slunný den.
yĕ SLOON-nee dĕn.

1878. It is windy (LIT.: **Wind is blowing**).
Fouká vítr.
FOH‿OO-kah VEE-tŭr.

1879. It is raining.
Prší.
PŬR-shee.

1880. It is snowing.
Sněží.
SNᵘĚ-zhee.

1881. Below freezing.
Pod bodem mrazu.
PAWD-baw-dĕm MRAH-zoo.

1882. The temperature.
Teplota.
TĚ-plaw-tah.

1883. I want to sit [in the shade].
Chci sedět [ve stínu].
khtsĭ SĚ-dᵘĕt [VĚ-stᵘee-noo].

1884. — in the sun. — na slunci.
— NAH-sloon-tsĭ.

1885. **I want to sit in a breeze** (LIT.: **I want the breeze to fan me**).

Chci, aby mě ovíval větřík.

khtsĭ, AH-bĭ mnᵁě AW-vēē-vahl VYĔT-rzheek.

1886. **What is the weather forecast [for tomorrow]?**

Jaká je předpověď počasí [na zítřek]?

YAH-kah yě PRZHĔT-paw-vyĕtᵁ PAW-chah-sēe [NAH-zēet-rzhĕk]?

1887. **— for the weekend** (LIT.: **for Saturday and Sunday**).

— na sobotu a neděli.

— NAH-saw-baw-too ah NĔ-dᵁě-lĭ.

DAYS OF THE WEEK
JMÉNA DNŮ V TÝDNU

1888. **Sunday.** Neděle. *NĔ-dᵁě-lě.*

1889. **Monday.** Pondělí. *PAWN-dᵁě-lēe.*

1890. **Tuesday.** Úterý. *ŌŌ-tě-rēe.*

1891. **Wednesday.** Středa. *STRZHĔ-dah.*

1892. **Thursday.** Čtvrtek. *CHTVŬR-těk.*

1893. **Friday.** Pátek. *PĀH-těk.*

1894. **Saturday.** Sobota. *SAW-baw-tah.*

HOLIDAYS
SVÁTKY

1895. A public holiday. Státní svátek.
$ST\overline{AH}T$-$n^{y}ee$ $SV\overline{AH}$-těk.

1896. Merry Christmas! Veselé vánoce!
$V\breve{E}$-sě-leh $V\overline{AH}$-naw-tsě!

1897. Easter. Velikonoce. $V\breve{E}$-lĭ-kaw-naw-tsě.

1898. Good Friday. Velký pátek. VEL-kee $P\overline{AH}$-těk.

1899. Happy New Year! Šťastný nový rok!
$SHT^{y}AHST$-nee NAW-vee rawk!

MONTHS AND SEASONS
MĚSÍCE A ROČNÍ OBDOBÍ

1900. January. Leden. $L\breve{E}$-děn.

1901. February. Únor. $\overline{OO}$-nawr.

1902. March. Březen. $BRZH\breve{E}$-zěn.

1903. April. Duben. DOO-běn.

1904. May. Květen. $KVY\breve{E}$-těn.

1905. June. Červen. $CH\breve{E}R$-věn.

1906. July. Červenec. $CH\breve{E}R$-vě-něts.

1907. August. Srpen. $S\breve{U}R$-pěn.

1908. **September.** Září. *ZĀH-rzhee.*

1909. **October.** Říjen. *RZHĒE-yĕn.*

1910. **November.** Listopad. *LĬS-taw-paht.*

1911. **December.** Prosinec. *PRAW-sĭ-nĕts.*

1912. **The spring.** Jaro. *YAH-raw.*

1913. **The summer.** Léto. *LĒH-taw.*

1914. **The autumn.** Podzim. *PAWD-zĭm.*

1915. **The winter.** Zima. *ZĬ-mah.*

NUMBERS: CARDINALS
ZÁKLADNÍ ČÍSLOVKY

1916. **One.** Jeden, jedna, jedno.
    YĔ-dĕn, YĔD-nah, YĔD-naw.

1917. **Two.** Dva, dvě. *dvah, dvyĕ.*

1918. **Three.** Tři. *trzhĭ.*

1919. **Four.** Čtyři. *CHTĬ-rzhĭ.*

1920. **Five.** Pět. *pyĕt.*

1921. **Six.** Šest. *shĕst.*

1922. **Seven.** Sedm. *SĔ-doom.*

1923. **Eight.** Osm. *AW-soom.*

1924. **Nine.** Devět. *DĔ-vyĕt.*

1925. **Ten.** Deset. *DĔ-sĕt.*

1926. Eleven. Jedenáct. *YĔ-dĕ-nāhtst.*

1927. Twelve. Dvanáct. *DVAH-nāhtst.*

1928. Thirteen. Třináct. *TRZHĬ-nāhtst.*

1929. Fourteen. Čtrnáct. *CHTŬR-nāhtst.*

1930. Fifteen. Patnáct. *PAHT-nāhtst.*

1931. Sixteen. Šestnáct. *SHĔST-nāhtst.*

1932. Seventeen. Sedmnáct. *SĔ-doom-nāhtst.*

1933. Eighteen. Osmnáct. *AW-soom-nāhtst.*

1934. Nineteen. Devatenáct. *DĔ-vah-tĕ-nāhtst.*

1935. Twenty. Dvacet. *DVAH-tsĕt.*

1936. Twenty-one. Jedenadvacet. *YĔ-dĕn-ah-dvah-tsĕt.*

1937. Twenty-two. Dvaadvacet. *DVAH-ah-dvah-tsĕt.*

1938. Thirty. Třicet. *TRZHĬ-tsĕt.*

1939. Thirty-one. Jedenatřicet.
YĔ-dĕn-ah-trzhĭ-tsĕt.

1940. Forty. Čtyřicet. *CHTĬ-rzhĭ-tsĕt.*

1941. Fifty. Padesát. *PAH-dĕ-sāht.*

1942. Sixty. Šedesát. *SHĔ-dĕ-sāht.*

1943. Seventy. Sedmdesát. *SĔ-doom-dĕ-sāht.*

1944. Eighty. Osmdesát. *AW-soom-dĕ-sāht.*

1945. Ninety. Devadesát. *DĔ-vah-dĕ-sāht.*

1946. (One) hundred. Sto. *staw.*

1947. One hundred and one. Sto jeden. *staw YĚ-děn.*

1948. One hundred and ten. Sto deset. *staw DĚ-sět.*

1949. (One) thousand. Tisíc. *T^{y}Ǐ-seets.*

1950. Two thousand. Dva tisíce. *dvah T^{y}Ǐ-see-tsě.*

1951. Three thousand. Tři tisíce. *trzhǐ T^{y}Ǐ-see-tsě.*

1952. Four thousand. Čtyři tisíce.
    CHTǏ-rzhǐ T^{y}Ǐ-see-tsě.

1953. Five thousand. Pět tisíc. *pyět T^{y}Ǐ-seets.*

1954. One hundred thousand. Sto tisíc.
    staw T^{y}Ǐ-seets.

1955. (One) million. Milión. *MǏ-li-yawn.*

NUMBERS: ORDINALS
ŘADOVÉ ČÍSLOVKY

1956. The first. První. *PǓRV-n^{y}ee.*

1957. The second. Druhý. *DROO-hee.*

1958. The third. Třetí. *TRZHĚ-t^{y}ee.*

1959. The fourth. Čtvrtý. *CHTVǓR-tee.*

1960. The fifth. Pátý. *PAH-tee.*

1961. The sixth. Šestý. *SHĚS-tee.*

1962. The seventh. Sedmý. *SĚD-mee.*

1963. The eighth. Osmý. *AWS-mee̅.*

1964. The ninth. Devátý. *DĔ-vah̅-tee̅.*

1965. The tenth. Desátý. *DĔ-sah̅-tee̅.*

1966. The twentieth. Dvacátý. *DVAH-tsah̅-tee̅.*

1967. The thirtieth. Třicátý. *TRZHĬ-tsah̅-tee̅.*

1968. The one hundredth. Stý. *stee̅.*

QUANTITIES
UDÁVÁNÍ MNOŽSTVÍ

1969. A fraction. Zlomek. *ZLAW-mĕk.*

1970. One quarter. Čtvrtina. *CHTVŬR-tᵘ ĭ-nah.*

1971. One third. Třetina. *TRZHĔ-tᵘ ĭ-nah.*

1972. One half. Polovina (OR: Půl).
PAW-law-vĭ-nah (OR: *pool̅).*

1973. Three quarters. Tři čtvrtiny.
trzhĭ CHTVŬR-tᵘ ĭ-nĭ.

1974. The whole. Celek. *TSĔ-lĕk.*

1975. A pair. Pár. *pah̅r.*

1976. A dozen. Tucet. *TOO-tsĕt.*

1977. A few. Pár (OR: Několik).
pah̅r (OR: *NᵘĔ-kaw-lĭk).*

1978. Several. Několik. *NᵘĔ-kaw-lĭk.*

1979. Many. Mnoho. *MNAW-haw.*

1980. More. Více. *V$\overline{EE}$-tsě.*

1981. Less. Méně. *M$\overline{EH}$-n^{y}ě.*

1982. Not enough. Málo. *M$\overline{AH}$-law.*

1983. Too much. Příliš hodně.
    PRZH$\overline{EE}$-lǐsh HAWD-n^{y}ě.

FAMILY
RODINA

1984. Wife. Manželka (OR: Žena).
    MAHN-zhěl-kah (OR: *ZHĚ-nah*).

1985. Husband. Manžel (OR: Muž).
    MAHN-zhěl (OR: *moosh*).

1986. Mother. Matka. *MAHT-kah.*

1987. Father. Otec. *AW-těts.*

1988. Grandmother. Babička. *BAH-bǐch-kah.*

1989. Grandfather. Dědeček. *D^{y}Ě-dě-chěk.*

1990. Daughter. Dcera. *TSĚ-rah.*

1991. Son. Syn. *sǐn.*

1992. Sister. Sestra. *SĚS-trah.*

1993. Brother. Bratr. *BRAH-tǔr.*

1994. Child. Dítě. *D$^y\overline{EE}$-t^{y}ě.*

1995. Children. Děti. *D ᵞĚ-t ᵞĭ.*

1996. Aunt. Teta. *TĚ-tah.*

1997. Uncle. Strýc. *streets.*

1998. Niece. Neteř. *NĚ-těrzh.*

1999. Nephew. Synovec. *SĬ-naw-věts.*

2000. Cousin. Bratranec. *BRAH-trah-něts.*

2001. Relative. Příbuzný. *PRZHEE-booz-nee.*

2002. Father-in-law. Tchán. *tkhahn.*

2003. Mother-in-law. Tchyně. *TKHĬ-n ᵞě.*

COMMON SIGNS AND PUBLIC NOTICES
BĚŽNÉ NÁPISY A VEŘEJNÁ OZNÁMENÍ

This section is alphabetized according to the Czech expressions, for convenience of reference to actual signs and notices you may see in your travels.

2004. Autobusová zastávka.
> *AH‿OO-taw-boo-saw-vah ZAH-stahf-kah.*
> Bus stop.

2005. Bezpečnost. *BĚS-pěch-nawst.* Police.

2006. Cizím vstup zakázán.
$\overline{TSI}$-zeem fstoop ZAH-ka$\overline{h}$-zahn.
No trespassing (LIT.: Access forbidden to
strangers).

2007. Čekárna. $CH\breve{E}$-ka$\overline{hr}$-nah. Waiting room.

2008. Čerstvý nátěr. $CH\breve{E}RS$-tvee $N\overline{AH}$-t^{y}ěr.
Wet (OR: Fresh) paint.

2009. Dál! $d\overline{ahl}$! Enter (OR: Come in).

2010. Dámský (OR: Ženský) záchod.
$D\overline{AHM}$-skee (OR: $ZH\breve{E}N$-skee) $Z\overline{AH}$-khawt.
Ladies' room.

2011. Dámy (OR: Ženy). $D\overline{AH}$-m$\breve{\imath}$ (OR: $ZH\breve{E}$-n$\breve{\imath}$).
Ladies.

2012. Dodržujte ticho!
DAW-dŭr-zhoo‿y-tě $T^y\breve{I}$-khaw.
No noise (OR: Keep quiet).

2013. Dolů. DAW-$\overline{loo}$. Down.

2014. Domovník. DAW-mawv-n$^y\overline{eek}$. Janitor.

2015. Dostavte se osobně.
DAW-stahf-tě-sě AW-sawb-n^{y}ě.
You are requested to come in person.

2016. Horký. $HAWR$-$\overline{kee}$. Hot.

2017. Hřbitov. $HRZHB\breve{I}$-tawf. Cemetery.

2018. Informace. $\breve{I}N$-fawr-mah-tsě. Information.

2019. (Jděte) opatrně! ($YD^y\breve{E}$-tě) AW-pah-tŭr-n^{y}ě!
Watch your step.

2020. Jídelna. *YĒE-děl-nah.* Diner (OR: Dining room).

2021. Jídelní vůz. *YĒE-děl-nʸee voos.* Dining car.

2022. K dostání zde. *GDAWS-tah-nʸee zdě.*
For sale here.

2023. Klinika. *KLĬ-nĭ-kah.* Clinic.

2024. Knihovna. *KNʸĬ-hawv-nah.* Library.

2025. Kosmetika. *KAWS-mě-tĭ-kah.* Cosmetics.

2026. Koupání zakázáno.
KOH‿OO-pah-nʸee ZAH-kah-zah-naw.
No swimming (OR: Bathing not allowed).

2027. Kouření dovoleno.
KOH‿OO-rzhě-nʸee DAW-vaw-lě-naw.
Smoking permitted.

2028. Kouření zakázáno.
KOH‿oo-rzhě-nʸee ZAH-kah-zah-naw.
Smoking forbidden.

2029. K pronajatí. *KPRAW-nah-yah-tʸee.*
For hire (OR: rent).

2030. Kuřák. *KOO-rzhahk.* Smoker.

2031. K vlakům. *KVLAH-koom.* To the trains.

2032. Muži. *MOO-zhĭ.* Men (OR: Gentlemen).

2033. Mužský záchod. *MOOSH-skee ZĀH-khawt.*
Men's room.

2034. Nahoru. *NAH-haw-roo.* Up.

2035. Nalevo. *NAH-lě-vaw.* To the left.

2036. Napravo. *NAH-prah-vaw.* To the right.

2037. Na prodej. *NAH-praw-day.* For sale.

2038. Nekrmit zvířata! *NĚ-kŭr-mĭt ZVĒĒ-rzhah-tah!*
Do not feed the animals.

2039. Nemocnice. *NĚ-mawts-nʸĭ-tsě.* Hospital.

2040. Neplivat! *NĚ-plĭ-vaht!* No spitting.

2041. Nepovolaným vstup zakázán.
NĚ-paw-vaw-lah-neem fstoop ZAH-kah-zahn.
No admittance except on business.

2042. Nepřetržitý provoz.
NĚ-přzhě-tŭr-zhĭ-tee PRAW-vaws.
Continuous performance.

2043. Nešlapat po trávě!
NĚ-shlah-paht PAW-trah-vyě!
Keep off the grass.

2044. Nouzový východ.
NOH‿OO-zaw-vee VĒĒ-khawt.
Emergency exit.

2045. Občerstvení. *AWP-chěrs-tvě-nʸee.*
Refreshments.

2046. Obchodní škola. *AWP-khawd-nʸee SHKAW-lah.*
Business school.

2047. Obsazeno. *AWP-sah-zě-naw.*
Occupied (or: Engaged).

2048. Odjezd. *AWD-yěst.* Departure.

2049. Odpadky. *AWT-paht-kĭ.* Refuse.

2050. Otevřeno. *AW-těv-rzhě-naw.* Open.

2051. **Otevřeno od osmi do půl dvanácté [dopo-ledne] večer.**

AW-tĕv-rzhĕ-naw   AWD-aws-mĭ   DAW-pool
DVAH-nāhts-teh [DAW-paw-lĕd-nĕ] VĚ-chĕr.
Open from 8 to 11:30 [A.M.] P.M.

2052. **Oznámení.** *AW-znah-mĕ-nʸee.* Notices.

2051. **Páni.** *PĀH-nʸĭ.* Men (OR: Gentlemen).

2054. **Pánský záchod.** *PĀHN-skee ZĀH-khawt.*
Men's room.

2055. **Podniková dovolená.**
PAWD-nʸĭ-kaw-vah DAW-vaw-lĕ-nah.
Closed for vacation.

2056. **Pokladna.** *PAW-khlad-nah.* Ticket office.

2057. **Polední přesnídávka.**
PAW-lĕd-nʸee PRZHĚ-snʸee-dahf-kah.
Lunch.

2058. **Poštovní schránka.**
PAWSH-tawv-nʸee SKHRĀHN-kah.
Mailbox.

2059. **[Pouze] pro chodce.**
[POH‿OO-zĕ] PRAW-khawt-tsĕ.
Pedestrians [only].

2060. **Pouze pro zaměstnance.**
POH‿OO-zĕ PRAW-zah-mnʸĕst-nahn-tsĕ.
Employees only.

2061. **Pozor, nebezpečí!** *PAW-zawr, NĚ-bĕs-pĕ-chee!*
Danger.

2062. (Pozor,) opravuje se!
  (*PAW-zwar,*) *AW-prah-voo-yĕ-sĕ!*
  Men at work.

2063. Pozor, zlý pes! *PAW-zawr, zlēe pĕs!*
  Beware of the dog.

2064. Představení se nekoná.
  PRZHĚT-stah-vĕ-n^yēe-sĕ NĚ-kaw-nah.
  No performance.

2065. Předprodej lístků.
  PRZHĚT-praw-day LĒEST-koo.
  Ticket office.

2066. Prodá se. *PRAW-dāh-sĕ.* For sale.

2067. Prodej. *PRAW-day.* Sale.

2068. Pronajme se dům. *PRAW-nah‿y-mĕ-sĕ dōom.*
  House for rent.

2069. Pronajmou se zařízené pokoje.
  PRAW-nah‿y-moh‿oo-sĕ   ZAH-rzhee-zĕ-neh
  PAW-kaw-yĕ.
  Furnished rooms for rent.

2070. Radnice. *RAHD-n^yĭ-tsĕ.* City hall.

2071. Rezervováno. *RĚ-zĕr-vaw-vāh-naw.* Reserved.

2072. Samoobsluha. *SAH-maw-awp-sloo-hah.*
  Self-service.

2073. Schody. *SKHAW-dĭ.* Stairs.

2074. Soukromá cesta. *SOH‿OO-kraw-mah TSĚS-tah.*
  Private road.

2075. Soukromý pozemek.
  SOH͜oo-kraw-mēe PAW-zĕ-mĕk.
  Private property.

2076. Stanoviště taxíků.
  STAH-naw-vĭsh-t͜ʸĕ TAH-ksēe-koo.
  Taxi stand.

2077. Studený. *STOO-dĕ-nēe.* Cold.

2078. Táhnout. *TĀH-hnoh͜oot.* Pull.

2079. Telefon. *TĔ-lĕ-fawn.* Telephone.

2080. Televize. *TĔ-lĕ-vĭ-zĕ.* Television.

2081. Ticho! *T͜ʸĬ-khaw!* Silence (OR: Quiet).

2082. Tlačit. *TLAH-chĭt.* Push.

2083. Továrna. *TAW-vāhr-nah.* Factory.

2084. Umělé chlazení vzduchu.
  OO-mn͜ʸĕ-lēh KHLAH-zĕ-n͜ʸee VZDOO-khoo.
  Air-conditioned.

2085. Vchod. *fkhawt.* Entrance.

2086. V drobném. *VDRAWB-nehm.* Retail.

2087. Veřejná bezpečnost.
  VĔ-rzhay-nāh BĔS-pĕch-nawst.
  Police.

2088. Veřejné oznámení.
  VĔ-rzhay-nēh AW-znāh-mĕ-n͜ʸee.
  Public notice.

2089. Veřejný telefon. *VĚ-rzhay-nee TĚ-lě-fawn.*
Public telephone.

2090. Ve velkém. *VĚ-věl-kehm.* Wholesale.

2091. Volno. *VAWL-naw.* Vacant.

2092. Vrátím se [v jedenáct hodin dopoledne] ve tři hodiny odpoledne.
VRĀH-tᵘeem-sě [VYĚ-dě-nāhtst HAW-dᵘin DAW-paw-lěd-ně] VĚ-trzhǐ HAW-dᵘǐ-nǐ AWT-paw-lěd-ně.
Will return [at 11 A.M.] at 3 P.M.

2093. Vrátný. *VRĀHT-nee.* Janitor.

2094. Vstupné. *FSTOOP-neh.* Admission.

2095. Vstupte. *FSTOOP-tě.* Come in.

2096. Vstup zakázán. *fstoop ZAH-kah-zahn.*
No admittance.

2097. Vstup zdarma. *fstoop ZDAHR-mah.*
Admission free.

2098. Vůz pro kuřáky. *voos PRAW-koo-rzhah-kǐ.*
Smoking car.

2099. Výhodná koupě. *VEE-hawd-nah KOH_OO-pyě.*
Bargain.

2100. Východ. *VEE-khawt.* Exit.

2101. Výtah. *VĒE-takh.* Elevator.

2102. Záchod. *ZĀH-khawt.* Toilet.

2103. Zakázáno. *ZAH-kah-zah-naw.*
Forbidden (OR: Prohibited).

2104. Zamluveno. *ZAH-mloo-vě-naw.*
Reserved.

2105. Zavřeno od dvanácti do dvou.
*ZAH-vrzhě-naw AWD-dvah-nahts-tʸĭ DAW-
dvoh‿oo.*
Closed from 12 to 2.

2106. Zavřeno v neděli a ve svátky.
ZAH-vrzhě-naw VNĚ-dʸě-lĭ ah VĚ-svaht-kĭ.
Closed on Sundays and holidays.

2107. Zdarma. *ZDAHR-mah.* Free.

2108. Zoologická zahrada (OR: Zoo).
ZAW-aw-law-gĭts-kah ZAH-hrah-dah (OR:
ZAW-aw).
Zoo.

2109. Zvonit. *ZVAW-nʸĭt.* Ring the bell.

2110. Železniční stanice.
ZHĚ-lěz-nʸĭch-nʸee STAH-nʸĭ-tsě.
Railroad station (OR: Depot).

Ženy: SEE **Dámy.**

ROAD SIGNS
DOPRAVNÍ ZNAČKY

This section contains a selection of the most important official Czech road signs, with the official Czech phrases they stand for.

2111.
Zatáčka vpravo.
ZAH-tahch-kah FPRAH-vaw.
Curve to the right.

2112.
Dvojitá zatáčka, první vlevo.
DVAW-yĭ-tah̄ ZAH-tahch-kah,
PŬRV-nʸee VLĔ-vaw.
Double curve, first to the left.

2113.
Křižovatka.
KRZHĬ-zhaw-vaht-kah.
Intersection.

2114.
Křižovatka s vedlejší silnicí.
KRZHĬ-zhaw-vaht-kah SVĔD-lay-
shee SĬL-nʸi-tsee.
Intersection of main and secondary roads.

2115.
Nebezpečné klesání.
NĔ-bĕs-pĕch-neh̄ KLĔ-sah-nʸee.
Dangerous slope.

2116.
Zúžená vozovka.
ZOO-zhĕ-nah VAW-zawf-kah.
Road narrows.

2117.
Příčná stružka nebo hrbol.
PRZHEECH-nah STROOSH-kah
NĔ-baw HŬR-bawl.
Bump.

2118.
Nebezpečí smyku.
NĔ-bĕs-pĕ-chee SMĬ-koo.
Danger of skidding.

2119.
Provoz v obou směrech.
PRAW-vaws VAW-boh_oo
SMNᵞĔ-rĕkh.
Two-way traffic.

2120.
Pozor, světelná znamení!
PAW-zawr, SVYĔ-tĕl-nah ZNAH-
mĕ-nᵞee!
Traffic signal ahead.

2121.
Železniční přejezd se závora-mi.
ZHĔ-lĕz-nᵞĭch-nᵞee PRZHĔ-yĕst
SĔ-zah-vaw-rah-mĭ.
Gated railroad crossing.

2122.

Železniční přejezd bez závor.

ZHĚ-lěz-n^{y}ích-n^{y}ee   PRZHĚ-yěst
BĚZ-zah-vawr.

Ungated railroad crossing.

2123.

Jiné nebezpečí.

YĬ-neh NĚ-běs-pě-chee.

Danger of other type.

2124.

Návěstní deska (160 m).

NĂH-vyěst-n^{y}ee DĚS-kah (staw
SHĚ-dě-saht MĚ-troo).

Approaching railroad crossing:
signal posted 160 meters before
crossing.

2125.

Výstražný kříž pro železniční
přejezd bez závor jednoko-
lejný.

VĒE-strahzh-nee krzheesh PRAW-
zhě-lěz-n^{y}ích-n^{y}ee PRZHĚ-yěst
BĚZ-zah-vawr YĚD-naw-kaw-
lay-nee.

Ungated railroad crossing (one
track).

2126.

Dej přednost v jízdě!

day PRZHĚD-nawst VYĒEZ-d^{y}ě!

Yield right of way.

2127.
Dej přednost v jízdě tramvaji!
day PRZHĚD-nawst   VYĒĒZ-d^vě
*   TRAHM-vah-yř!*
Yield right of way to streetcar.

2128.
Stůj, dej přednost v jízdě!
stoo‿y,   day   PRZHĚD-nawst
*   VYĒĒZ-d^vě!*
Stop, yield right of way.

2129.
Zákaz vjezdu všech vozidel
(v obou směrech).
ZĀH-kahs VYĚZ-doo fshěkh VAW-
*   zř-děl (VAW-boh‿oo SMN^yĚ-*
*   řekh).*
Do not enter (applicable to all
    vehicles); entry forbidden in
    both directions.

2130.
Zákaz vjezdu všech vozidel.
ZĀH-kahs VYĚZ-doo fshěkh VAW-
*   zř-děl.*
Do not enter (applicable to all
    vehicles).

2131.

Zákaz vjezdu všech motorových vozidel s výjimkou motocyklů bez postranního vozíku.

ZĀH-kahs VYĚZ-doo fshěkh MAW-taw-raw-vēekh VAW-zĭ-děl SVĒE-yĭm-koh‿oo MAW-taw-tsĭ-kloo BĚS-paw-strahn-nᵛee-haw VAW-zee-koo.

Entry forbidden to all motor vehicles except motorcycles without sidecars.

2132.

Zákaz vjezdu všech motorových vozidel.

ZĀH-kahs VYĚZ-doo fshěkh MAW-taw-raw-vēekh VAW-zĭ-děl.

Do not enter (applicable to all motor vehicles).

2133.

Zákaz vjezdu vozidel, jejichž skutečná váha přesahuje vyznačenou mez.

ZĀH-kahs VYĚZ-doo VAW-zĭ-děl, YĚ-yĭkhsh SKOO-těch-nāh VĀH-hah PRZHĚ-sah-hoo-yě VĬZ-nah-chě-noh‿oo měs.

Entry forbidden to vehicles whose actual weight exceeds the limit shown [in this case, six metric tons, or 6000 kg].

2134.
Zákaz vjezdu vozidel, jejichž celková šířka přesahuje vyznačenou mez.

ZĀH-kahs VYĚZ-doo VAW-zĭ-děl, YE-yĭkhsh TSĚL-kaw-vah SHĒERZH-kah PRZHĚ-sah-hoo-yě VĬZ-nah-chě-noh_oo měs.

Entry forbidden to vehicles whose actual width exceeds the limit shown [in this case, 2.5 metres]

2135.
Omezená rychlost.

AW-mě-zě-nah RĬKH-lawst.

Speed limit [30 kilometers per hour].

2136.
Konec omezené rychlosti.

KAW-něts AW-mě-zě-neh RĬKH-laws-tʸĭ.

End of speed limit.

2137.
Zákaz předjíždění.

ZĀH-kahs PRZHĚD-yeezh-dʸě-nʸee.

Passing forbidden.

2138.
Konec zákazu předjíždění.

KAW-něts   ZĀH-kah-zoo
PRZHĚD-yēēzh-dᵛě-nᵛee.

End of zone in which passing is
forbidden.

2139.
Zákaz zvukových výstražných
znamení.

ZĀH-kahs ZVOO-kaw-vēēkh VĒE-
strahzh-neekh ZNAH-mě-nᵛee.

Sounding horn prohibited.

2140.
Zákaz odbočování vpravo.

ZĀH-kahs   AWD-baw-chaw-vāh-
nᵛee FPRAH-vaw.

No right turn.

2141.
Zákaz otáčení.

ZĀH-kahs AW-tah-chě-nᵛee.

No U-turn.

2142.
Dej přednost v jízdě protije-
doucím vozidlům!

day PRZHĚD-nawst VYĒEZ-dᵛě
PRAW-tᵛĭ-yě-doh_oo-tseem
VAW-zĭd-lōom.

Yield right of way to vehicles
moving in opposite direction.

2143.
Stůj, celní úřad!
stoo‿y, TSĚL-nʸee OO-rzhaht!
Stop, customs.

2144.
Zákaz zastavení.
ZAH-kahs ZAH-stah-vě-nʸee.
No stopping.

2145.
Zákaz stání.
ZAH-kahs STAH-nʸee.
No standing (No parking).

2146.
Střídavé stání.
STRZHEE-dah-veh STAH-nʸee.
Alternate street standing (Alternate street parking).

2147.
Přikázaný směr jízdy.
PRZHĬ-kah-zah-nee smnʸěr YEEZ-dĭ.
Drive in the direction shown.

2148.
Kruhový objezd.
KROO-haw-vee AWB-yěst.
Traffic circle.

2149.
Nejnižší dovolená rychlost.
NAY-nʸĭsh-sheē DAW-vaw-lĕ-nah RĬKH-lawst.
Minimum speed [30 km per hr].

2150.
Stezka pro chodce.
STĔS-kah PRAW-khawt-tsĕ.
Path for pedestrians.

2151.
Jednosměrný provoz.
YĔD-naw-smnʸĕr-neē PRAW-vaws.
One-way traffic.

2152.
Slepá ulice.
SLĔ-pah OO-lĭ-tsĕ.
Dead-end.

2153.
Parkoviště.
PAHR-kaw-vĭsh-tʸĕ.
Parking lot.

2154.
Nemocnice.
NĔ-mawts-nʸĭ-tsĕ.
Hospital.

2155.
Stanice první pomoci.
STAH-nʸĭ-tsĕ PŬRV-nʸee PAW-maw-tsĭ.
First aid station.

2156.
Opravna.
AW-prahv-nah.
Service station.

2157.
Tábořiště pro stany a obytné přívěsy.
TĀH-baw-rzhĭsh-tᵘě   PRAW-stah-nĭ ah AW-bĭt-nēh   PRZHĒE-vᵘĕ-sĭ.
Campsite for tents and trailers.

INDEX

All the sentences, words and phrases in this book are numbered consecutively from 1 to 2157. The entries in this index refer to these numbers. In addition, each major section heading (capitalized) is indexed according to page number. Parts of speech are indicated (where there might be confusion) by the following italic abbreviations: *adj.* for adjective, *adv.* for adverb, *n.* for noun, *prep.* for preposition, and *v.* for verb. Parentheses are used for explanations.

Because of the already large extent of the indexed material, cross-indexing has been avoided. Phrases or groups of two words or more will be found under only one of their components (e.g., "express train" only under "express," even though there is a separate entry for "train" alone). If you do not find a phrase under one of its words, try another.

Every English word or phrase in the index is followed by its Czech equivalent, which is usually given in its dictionary form (the nominative singular of nouns, pronouns and adjectives, and the infinitive of verbs; participles and verbal nouns have been listed separately). Thus, in effect, the reader is here provided with a basic

English–Czech glossary of up-to-the-minute language. Naturally, an acquaintance with Czech grammar is essential for making the best use of this index, since Czech is a highly inflected language. To assist you in using the correct forms of words in sentences of your own making, the index lists not only the first numbered sentence in which each word occurs, but also the sentences in which the word occurs with a different ending.

Thus, for example, under "want," sentences 100, 254, 278 and 1154 are listed for the Czech verb *chtít*. These sentences (in numerical order) provide the forms *chci* (I want), *chtěl bych* (I [would] want), *chceme* (we want) and *chtěli bychom* (we [would] want)—in other words, all the different forms of *chtít* that happen to appear in the book. Invariable words are indexed only under their first appearance, and only one appearance of each variation is given, so that there are no unnecessary duplicate listings. The beginner would do well to look at all the sentences listed for a Czech word in order to become familiar with the range of variations (and at all the Czech equivalents listed for an English word to become familiar with their different shades of meaning).

It is of course not the purpose of the present book to supply all possible inflectional endings or to teach you Czech grammar. But it will give you the proper form to look up in a dictionary, where you will find further information.

Where a numbered sentence contains a choice

of Czech equivalents (e.g., sentence 12, which gives *možná* or *snad* for "perhaps"), only the first choice has been included in the index. (Always refer to the sentences for more information).